THE NEW AGE OF AGEING

THE NEW AGE OF AGEING

How society needs to change

Caroline Lodge, Eileen Carnell and Marianne Coleman

First published in Great Britain in 2016 by

Policy Press
University of Bristol
1-9 Old Park Hill
Bristol
BS2 8BB
UK
t: +44 (0)117 954 5940
pp-info@bristol.ac.uk
www.policypress.co.uk

North America office:
Policy Press
c/o The University of Chicago Press
1427 East 60th Street
Chicago, IL 60637, USA
t: +1 773 702 7700
f: +1 773 702 9756
sales@press.uchicago.edu
www.press.uchicago.edu

British Library Cataloguing in Publication Data
A catalogue record for this book is available from the British Library.

Library of Congress Cataloging-in-Publication Data
A catalog record for this book has been requested.

ISBN 978-1-4473-2683-0 paperback
ISBN 978-1-4473-2685-4 ePub
ISBN 978-1-4473-2686-1 Mobi

The right of Caroline Lodge, Eileen Carnell and Marianne Coleman to be identified as authors of this work has been asserted by them in accordance with the Copyright, Designs and Patents Act 1988.

Cover design by Soapbox Design
Printed and bound in Great Britain by TJ International, Padstow
Policy Press uses environmentally responsible print partners

Contents

List of figures and tables

Figures

Tables

Acknowledgements

We would like to thank all who took part in our research and provided material for our book, in particular the 50 people whose interview responses have made such a rich contribution. We would also like to thank those we consulted about specific issues who generously shared their particular area of expertise.

We are grateful to the many readers of draft chapters, especially Professor Alex Moore, Professor Ann Briggs, Lynda Haddock and Sarah Grylls for reading all, or most, of the chapters and providing such helpful feedback and encouragement. Other readers included our friends, families and colleagues. Thanks are also due to Isobel Larkin for her inspiration, support and invaluable help as a source of research and connections. Thanks to Anna Lodge, Dave Chapman and Frances Northrop for specialist assistance. We would like to thank our retiring women's group: Jennifer Evans, Anne Gold, Allie Kirton and Anne Peters, who provide an important forum for discussion and support.

Finally, we would like to thank all those at Policy Press who provided guidance and encouragement: Policy Press publisher and editor Alison Shaw, Jessica Miles for the publicity, the publishing executive Laura Vickers, and Judith Oppenheimer for copy editing, Soapbox Design for the cover design, and colleagues in the production team.

About the authors

Caroline Lodge works as a freelance writer, coach and active grandmother. As an academic she has researched learning in schools and is skilled in presenting research material to others.

Eileen Carnell is a writer and consultant. Her main research focus is on learning. She works in many different settings to support adults' and young people's learning, especially in the arts.

Marianne Coleman has continued to research and write since retirement and has a particular interest in gender and leadership. She has written extensively on diversity issues.

List of abbreviations

BMJ   British Medical Journal
DRA   Default Retirement Age
GDP   Gross Domestic Product
HALE   Health Adjusted Life Expectancy
OECD   Organisation for Economic Co-operation and Development
ONS   Office for National Statistics
SPA   State Pension Age
TUC   Trades Union Congress
U3A   University of the Third Age
WHO   World Health Organization

ONE

The new age of ageing: how society needs to change

A former nurse, aged 75, attracted much attention in the press in the summer of 2015 when she announced her decision to end her life at a clinic in Switzerland. In her statement 'My Last Word', Gill Pharaoh raised many issues, not least about the morality and practicalities of ending her own life.[1] Despite being fit and well when she made her decision, Gill

- saw old age as a state of deterioration;
- hated the possibility of dependence on others;
- believed that she would become someone else in old age;
- thought life in old age was less attractive than death.

We are living in a new age of ageing, and we call it this because so many more people are living for longer. Life expectancy is rising everywhere. The population profile is changing, with consequences for us all, not just for older people. Gill Pharaoh's view of old age illustrates one individual's response to growing older.

We are concerned, in this book, about the reactions to this new age, not just at an individual level but in every aspect of our lives. For some time we three authors, all in our 60s when this writing began, have questioned taken-for-granted assertions about old age. We have also noticed ageism in many walks of life and realised that social policy frequently fails to address the needs raised by increased longevity. We have explored and extended our understanding of what it means to get older in our world. We are committed to ideals of inclusion, social justice and equity in an increasingly diverse society. We have drawn on our experiences as feminists to look at ageing differently, envisage action for improvement and look at how society needs to change.

Gill Pharaoh's testament indicates many questions about ageing that we have been examining. There is the experience of the physicality of ageing, what it means to live in our bodies as they grow older. How do the processes of ageing change us and make us different, and in what ways do we remain unchanged? How do we make sense of our relationship to others in the world as we age? What do our families owe us, or what can we expect from them, and they from us? Above all, we found it harder and harder to accept without questioning the negative assumptions that abound about ageing and about the consequences of an increased number of older people. Reading and research further confirmed and justified our stance.

We present some alternative ways of thinking, talking and planning about ageing: a new paradigm of an age-inclusive society. We challenge current assumptions about ageing and exclusionary practices towards older people, to build a case for improvements in policy and planning, and changes in attitudes and beliefs about ageing and older people.

Why this book matters

More people are living longer. Our book is particularly concerned with three outcomes of increased longevity:

2

the changes that will result, the lack of awareness of these changes and the negative responses to the increased number of older people.

The first consequence is that changes will be pervasive. However, the extent and scope of the changes are poorly understood, under-estimated or ignored. Some outcomes will have an impact at a personal level as individuals and their closest circles make sense of increasing longevity and the changes to relationships and obligations that this will bring. The changes will also be experienced at a wider social level, affecting how neighbourhoods and communities live together and how care is provided for those most in need. And there are economic challenges: the costs and benefits of extended lives, and changes to the commercial world and the workplace so as to adapt to older consumers and workers. These are very large social and economic changes.

The second consequence is that a lack of knowledge about these changes means a failure to prepare for them. There is a delay between the changes' occurring and their implications' being absorbed by individuals and by society. As a result, actions and reactions are often based on out-of-date information and ideas. An example of this is the way that the demographic change is viewed as catastrophic – the phrase often used is 'time bomb'. This idea draws on the belief that everyone over 65 will be dependent upon the decreasing proportion of those under 65. This assumption is out of date, yet influential in social and economic discussion.

There is an increasing amount of research and data about our society and the effects of the ageing population, in particular from scholars in the field of social gerontology, the New Dynamics of Ageing Research project, Age UK, dementia support organisations and others undertaking research. We notice some shifts as the research finds its way into newspapers and investigative TV programmes. Soaps and popular TV programmes have been more willing to include

3

older characters and people with dementia. Despite these welcome developments, public discourse largely takes place in ignorance of the changes we explore in this book. We aim to present up-to-date information and research in this book in order to inform discussions about demographic change.

Our third concern is the expression of negative and ageist attitudes towards older people that extends beyond the disappearance of older women from TV screens, although that is an important example. We have noticed that prejudiced attitudes towards older people are still socially acceptable in a way that prejudices against other groups are not and that these attitudes are reproduced in humour, political comment, employment practices and social life. Some responses go further and blame older people for the outcomes of the demographic change.

In addition to denigrating attitudes, we have also detected widespread denial. In popular discussion about ageing, language is used to imply that ageing is happening only to other people, to older people. Yet we all begin to age from birth, and everyone who survives will become an older person. People who are older are not a separate category. The survival of more people for longer and in better health is going to change the future for everyone, no matter what their age. For example, increasing life expectancy means that youth goes on for longer and that decisions about having children are more likely to be delayed.

We have already noted the tendency to assume that ageing is what happens to other people, and we are aware that many people would include us within the category of older people, as all three of us are older than 65. Although we have tried, we ourselves have not always been able to avoid referring to older people as 'them', as if they are other than ourselves, despite wanting to present an ideal of an age-inclusive society. Ageing is a process common to everyone, but it needs saying that people experience ageing differently. It needs saying because those over 65 are often lumped together as if they come from the same generation and have the same needs and ambitions. There may be up to three generations who fit the description of older people. Gender, class, income, ethnicity, country of origin, sexuality, family status, state of health, mental history and other variations in life each imply difference: older people area as diverse as the population as a whole.

As we three authors entered our 60s and move into our 70s we have become more aware of simplistic and ageist attitudes towards older people. We have all been involved in fighting for inclusion and equity in a diverse society – for example, the struggle against sexism – and can draw on a critical understanding of how society can discriminate against a particular group and what we might do to change such attitudes. With three lifetimes of social research and social and political action between us, we find that we need to speak out – about inequalities, lack of informed debate, unexplored assumptions, prejudices and the treatment of older people in the UK today.

We have not come across another book that brings together research and the voices of older people to challenge, and to envision a different future for, our society. We write for a variety of readers who share an interest in social issues and in finding out more about the world in which we live. We argue for an inclusive response and therefore hope that our readership will be of all ages. We expect many of our readers to be from our generation, entering their 60s and 70s. We are more diverse, healthier, better educated and more willing to be politically involved and to challenge prejudice than previous generations were. Many of us have the belief that a better society can be created by our own efforts.

Themes of the book

Impacts on four layers of society

One way in which we have made sense of the implications for the new age of ageing is to consider the outcomes at one or more of these levels of society:

- individual
- family
- community or neighbourhood
- society as a whole.

We are faced with questions and challenges at each level.

How are *individuals* to consider the changes in longevity? What challenges and prejudices does the individual face? Is old age to be approached with fear or with confidence? What are the opportunities of old age? What are the gains and losses?

How are *families* to respond to the implications of their loved ones living longer, needing accommodation, care and attention? What should be expected of them by the state or in cultural terms? How do families benefit from having great-grandparents? And what of those who have no children?

In *local communities* how can the potential benefits be realised? Will the opportunity to enjoy the unique contributions of older people be grasped? Will there be more or less segregation, especially in accommodation? How will neighbourhoods support their older inhabitants?

Society as a whole needs to grasp the emerging policy issues relating to health, care, housing, financial support and the workforce. What is to be done about continuing discriminatory practices on the grounds of age, despite their being illegal? Are older people to be seen as a burden or as a resource? One report suggests that five areas need immediate policy changes: support to the more disadvantaged; information to help individuals to plan for longer lives; funding for health and social care; facilitation of longer working lives; building more houses.[2] Society needs to change.

There is also a *global* aspect to increased longevity, as it is an international phenomenon. We focus on the UK, but at times also consider parallel experience in other countries. Different cultural practices have led to approaches that contrast with the UK's responses. And they give us hope that if things are done differently in other countries, we also can change. We have avoided romanticising ideas about the care of elders or the wisdom of the senior generation.

Themes

Our book presents the possibility of a better society, an age-inclusive society that values older people. We do not find this view comprehensively explored elsewhere. Here is how we build the picture.

The focus of the next chapter is on the all-important facts and figures about demographic changes. It is followed by a chapter that explores how ageing is viewed in the UK today and examines the ideas and theories that have framed dominant views. We consider why ageing and old people are seen as problems and challenges. We put the case that conceptions of ageing are socially constructed and therefore can change. We draw attention to ageist concepts, expose them and introduce some alternative ideas, including thinking differently about the lifecourse and about age-inclusivity.

Dependency dominates economic discussion, as well as issues such as care and family relationships. In Chapter Four we debunk the idea of a demographic time bomb resulting from increased dependence. We argue that political ideology is orchestrating a trend, with the intent to set what are often termed the older and greedy generation against the younger generation. Rather than running away from the so-called time bomb, which has been ticking away for a quarter of a century, we recommend preparation for the changes that increased longevity is bringing.

Throughout the book we identify the exclusionary practices that marginalise older people and present alternative approaches based on new information about our ageing society: the overlooked consumer (Chapter Five); practices that discriminate against older people, especially in employment and the media (Chapters Six and Seven); the pressures on people to adapt their appearance and to cover signs of ageing (Chapter Eight); issues in housing and care (Chapters Nine and Ten).

The voices of our interviewees are essential to Chapter Eleven, which explores the more challenging aspects of ageing. (In the next section we explain more about these interviews, which we have used throughout.) We consider our interviewees' understanding of death and illness for themselves and their loved ones. We also acknowledge that a substantial proportion of older people live in relative poverty and that loneliness and depression are the adjuncts of ageing for some.

We consider the benefits of ageing in Chapter Twelve, in order to combat the dominant images of decline and misery that are associated with growing older: how older people are continuing to learn, develop new identities and strengthen relationships, have fun and enjoy themselves.

We have examined the idea of wisdom in old age in Chapter Thirteen, but do not adopt a romantic or sentimental idea that age confers wisdom. Instead we look at the potential for experience to add to knowledge and for people to act more wisely together in social situations. We argue against the segregation of older people from social, political and community practices, because we believe that we should encourage reflection on experience and make better use of the resulting wisdom. The value of elder wisdom for age-inclusive practices is a theme that permeates this book.

In the penultimate chapter we celebrate those older people who are still actively involved in arguing, campaigning and working towards a better society for everyone, and especially for older people. We demonstrate that older people continue to be activists and subversives while retaining power, dignity and courage. The chapter titled 'We're still here' claims the political ground for older people.

At the end of each chapter we identify what needs to change in order that we can deal with the consequences of an ageing population. In the final chapter we draw these thoughts together in an invitation to readers to join us in action to promote a better future.

How the book was written

From an early stage in writing this book we wanted to include the voices of older people alongside our own. This is, of course, in keeping with the vision the book presents. Our intention is to be inclusive, not to objectify older people or treat them as different or 'other'. The authors undertook interviews with more than 50 people aged from 50 to 90. The interviews were mainly based on a set of questions that gave us the opportunity to talk with people. A few were specialist interviews drawing on a particular expertise. In some cases the specialists are named, with their agreement. In most cases we have given pseudonyms to our interviewees and we indicate their age at the time we spoke to them in order to give a small amount of context for their experiences. We also have drawn on the comments of our first-draft readers, who often added new dimensions.

We do not claim that our interview selection is representative of all older people. We doubt whether a representative sample is achievable. The people we spoke to are, on the whole, educated – that is, they have university degrees or professional qualifications. They are not all affluent, or female, or British, or healthy, although many of them are.

We have used these interviews in three ways. First, we identify current perspectives on ageing by those who are most affected; second, we draw themes about particular topics from the interviews; and third, we create a source of authentic voices to illustrate points of view, experiences, challenges, views and suggestions.

We also owe a large debt to those engaged in research, especially to social gerontologists. We recognise that many of our perspectives will be very familiar to people working in that field. We wish to make their work more available to the wider public so as to better inform discussions.

We do not want to live in a society where someone approaching old age considers that suicide is a better option than ageing. The majority of people are happiest and experience the highest levels of well-being between the ages of 65 and 79.[3] So we know that ageing can be so much more than an experience of deterioration; that dependence upon others is being delayed; that we can promote an understanding of old age as part of life's course, not a strange place that we enter as an alien; that we can imagine and work towards a society that does not segregate and discriminate against its oldest members.

Throughout our professional lives, the three authors have been committed to equity and inclusion, making the world better through education, research and writing. We have extended these experiences to argue for a better future for older people in Britain – one informed by research and one that argues for taking account of the changes that have already begun. And we know that our vision indicates that a better future for older people, which is better for everyone, is achievable. In short, we are capable of living better together for longer in this new, older world.

TWO

Going on and on

As mentioned in Chapter One, the term 'demographic time bomb' is often used in relation to the ageing population; we unpick and challenge this emotive phrase in detail in Chapter Four. In this chapter we look at the demographic changes in order to consider what they are, their scale and scope and their social implications.

We are certainly facing deep-seated changes of a type never experienced before – even if the term time bomb is not accurate, since it implies something that is a one-off occurrence. What we are experiencing is an on-going trend. We will not revert to a 'normal' pattern of population growth and distribution. Rather, we are seeing the establishment of a different pattern in which it looks as if life expectancy will continue to increase. Some geneticists claim that in the relatively near future technology to repair and renew cells could bring about vast increases in life expectancy, even up to 1,000 years.[1] This chapter sets the scene for the rest of the book by presenting the main facts and figures about how the age profile of the population of the UK, Europe and the rest of the world is changing; and the causes of the change that will affect us and involve a re-evaluation of many aspects of life for the individual, their family, their community and for society.

Why is the population ageing?

There are two overwhelming reasons why we have an ageing population. The most important is that the death rate is slowing, due to medical advances and better living conditions in much of the world. A second reason is that, generally, the birth rate has gone down too. More people are living to old age and fewer people are being born, so that in most countries the proportion of older people to young is growing.

If we take the example of the UK we can see how things are changing and are expected to continue changing (Table 2.1).

Table 2.1: The ageing population

	1985	2010	2035
Percentage of people aged 65 and over	15%	17%	23%
Percentage of people aged 85 and over	1%	2%	5%

Source: ONS (2015a) *Ageing of the UK Population* (accessed 10 August 2015)

In contrast to the growing proportion of over 65s, the proportion of those of aged 16–64 will reduce from nearly 65% of the UK population in 2012 to a forecast 59% in 2035.[2] The typical shape of the population 'pyramid' has given way to a more 'rectangular' shape in many countries, particularly in the Western world (Figures 2.1 and 2.2).

Figure 2.1: A traditionally shaped population pyramid, where the young outnumber the old

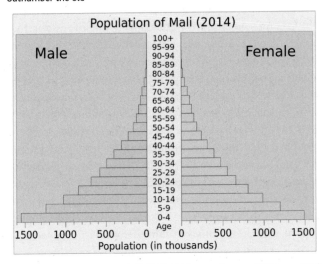

Source: Delphi234 Wikimedia.org/wiki/File%3AMalipop.svg (accessed 29 February 2016)

Figure 2.2: A 'rectangularised' population pyramid, where more people are living longer and older generations outnumber the younger generations. This shape is now typical of developed countries

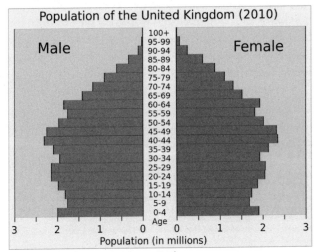

Source: Delphi234 (accessed 29 February 2016)

Just who is living longer?

On average, we are all living longer, but life is not that simple. If we just take the UK as an example, the changes are not uniform across the whole country. The median age, which is that point where half the population is older and half is younger, has changed in the UK from just over 35 years in 1985 to nearly 40 years in 2010 and is expected to go up to 42 years by 2035.[3] However, England and Northern Ireland have a younger median population than Wales and Scotland. London has a younger age profile than the rest of England. Why would that be? Two factors in particular account for the variations. One is a continuing higher birth rate in Northern Ireland because of the impact of religion, and the other is the impact of immigration in England, and particularly in London, which tends to attract people of working age, who are also those who are having children. Life expectancy varies in different regions too, with Scotland generally having poorer figures than the rest of the UK. The contrasts are stark between the regions.[4] Class, income and occupation all play a really important part in how long individuals live. Both men and women in the UK born into the richest families can expect to live on average seven years longer than those born into the poorest families, and these differences can be seen regionally as in Table 2.2.

Table 2.2: Differences in life expectancy at birth (2012)

	Men	Women
Glasgow	72.6	78.5
East Dorset	82.9	86.6

Source: ONS (2015b) *Life Expectancy at Birth and at Age 65 by local areas in England and Wales 2012 to 2014*, http://www.ons.gov.uk/peoplepopulationandcommunity/birthsdeathsandmarriages/lifeexpectancies/bulletins lifeexpectancyatbirthandatage65bylocalareasinenglandandwales/2015-11-04 (accessed 29 January 2016)

As well as the large difference between these two contrasting regions, Table 2.2 illustrates the well-known difference in the life expectancy of men and women, another factor that affects the ageing population. In the UK, currently life expectancy for a male born in 2012 is 79 years, and for a female it is 82.7 years. If current trends continue, by 2037 a further five years will have been added to life expectancy. At that rate it is possible that one in three of the babies born in 2013 will live until age 100. At the start of the chapter we mentioned that demographic changes would mean that we would all have to re-evaluate. Have we fully thought about the consequences for individuals, communities and society as a whole in a population where one in three people might live to be centenarians?

Along with the overall trend for both sexes to live longer, the extent of the difference in life expectancy of men and women is changing slightly, as the life expectancy of men is increasing at a faster rate than is that of women.[5] If this particular trend continues it will mean that by 2030 life expectancy for men and women in the UK will be equal. This would be quite a contrast to earlier days – for example, to 1969, when the difference in life expectancy for men and women peaked at 5.7 years. The current trend is mainly to do with the narrowing of differences in life-style between men and women, with fewer men smoking and doing manual work and more women taking part in the workforce; but have we thought about the implications of there being increasing numbers of older men? The evidence suggests that women tend to be more resilient when it comes to living alone, as so many older people do, and single old men are particularly likely to suffer from loneliness.[6]

What about the birth rate (and its bulges)?

The main reason for an ageing population is that more people are living longer. But it is not the only reason. The number of children born and surviving also affects the average age of the population, and therefore the rate at which it is ageing overall. Life expectancy is greater for all of us, including the new-born. An example from recent years is that in 2013 the infant mortality rate in England and Wales was 3.8 per 1,000 live births, as compared with 4.0 per 1,000 live births in 2012 and 10.1 per 1,000 live births as recently as 1983.[7]

The historical trend of the birth rate has been downwards since Victorian times. However, trends are not necessarily smooth and there are times when the birth rate has differed from the overall trend. The highest birth rate ever recorded was in 1920, after the First World War.[8] However, this increase was not sustained, unlike the famous 'bulge' in the birth rate after the Second World War, which was caused by couples delaying having a child until the war had ended. The relatively low birth rate during the Second World War was followed by a baby boom in the latter part of the 1940s and start of the 1950s, and the effects were quite dramatic. To take a small but typical example, one of the authors' secondary schools, Lawnswood High School in Leeds, normally had a three-form entry of 30 pupils each year, but in 1957 it was necessary to create an additional form to accommodate the children born in 1945/46. But that was not the end of it, as in 1958 a second additional form was provided for children born in 1946/47, so that in 1958 the annual intake of the school rose to 150, rather than the usual 90. The intake remained high for the next few years and then fell before a second peak in the 1960s. This pattern was repeated across the UK. In contrast to these two 'bulges' in the UK, the post-war bulge of the so-called baby boomers in the US simply continued from 1945 until the mid-1960s.

Those who were born in the UK and other countries during those boom years are now reaching pension age and adding to the underlying trend of an ageing population. The 1960s' bulge in the birth rate in the UK will also contribute to the growing proportion of the older generation. But the post-war changes in the birth rate are not the cause of the ageing population now; they just exacerbate the underlying trend that was and is happening anyway.

More recently there has been a blip in the birth rate that actually goes against the overall downward trend that contributes to an ageing population. In the UK, unlike elsewhere in Europe, the birth rate has been going up since 2000, even though it still remains below replacement level, which is the point where birth rates and death rates are equal. This small rise in the birth rate just goes to confirm that trends are never smooth and gives us a hint that the best-founded forecasts may turn out to be wrong.

A revolution for women

The huge changes in the lives of women in the UK and other Western countries over the last 100 years have had an impact on the ageing of the population. The ability of women to control their fertility has led to the fall in the birth rate, which in turn is related to the other major change for women, the growth in their numbers working outside the home. Although this trend was interrupted in the UK after the end of the Second World War, when women were encouraged to go back to the home, it resumed after the second wave of feminism and was supported by a raft of legislation in the 1970s giving women the right to equal pay, protection against discrimination and the opportunity for paid maternity leave.

If we go back to 1971, in England only 53% of women aged 16–64 were in paid employment, but by 2011 this had changed to 67%, fairly comparable with the 76% of men who were working.[9] This change of focus for women, from home to work, has changed our view of women and families and impacted on the birth rate, and being child free is becoming more common. Nine out of ten women born in the 1940s had a child or children, against eight out of ten women who were born in 1967,[10] and this trend may continue as women delay decisions about motherhood, but we need to be aware that the increasing number of childless couples will impact on the support and care of older people in the future.

Moving populations

A factor that has an impact on the population and its average age is the extent to which people enter and leave the country. The difference between the two is net migration, and the figures for net migration into the UK have been relatively high in recent years. Between 1991 and 2012 there was an increase in the UK population of four million people, half of which was due to net migration.[11] Most people who migrate do so for economic reasons and so they tend to be of working age and therefore of child-bearing age. The relatively young age of many immigrants to the UK has contributed to bringing down the median age of the population and added to the working-age population, countering the overall trend of ageing as well as contributing to economic growth. The impact of immigration is often seen, at least in the popular press, in negative terms, but the immigrant population impacts positively on the age profile of the UK, as well as sustaining much of the current caring workforce – with implications for the care of older people.

So far we have been focusing on the ageing population of the UK. To summarise:

- the main cause of the ageing population is increasing life expectancy;
- the generally lower birth rate has contributed to there being an ageing population;
- the lower birth rate in turn has been influenced by changes in the lives of women;
- the post-Second World War baby boom has contributed to, but not caused, the ageing population;
- net migration has had a mitigating effect on the rate at which the population is ageing.

Looking wider

If we look wider than the UK, to the EU, the picture relating to the ageing population is much the same, although the trends are even more pronounced in many of the other EU countries than they are in the UK. The birth rate has been slightly higher in the UK than in many other European countries since 2000 and, as we have seen, net migration plays a part. As a result the UK, which was the most 'aged' country in the EU in 1985, is now set to be one of the 'youngest'. In 2010, 17% of the UK population were over 65, while the proportion in Germany was already 21%. By 2035, the UK population over 65 will be one of the smallest in the EU, at 23%, while the proportion in Germany will be 31%.[12] However, in this dynamic world, recent waves of immigration into Germany and other European countries are changing the picture.

Looking beyond Europe, to the international position, the same story of an ageing population applies, and not only in developed countries but also in those that are developing. We think of the ageing population as being an issue in the Western world, but in fact the ageing of the population is happening faster in developing countries than anywhere else. The World Health Organization (WHO) tells us that in the first half of the 21st century the proportion of people in the world aged 60 or over will roughly double, from 11% to 22%, and it is in the low- to middle-income countries that the fastest growth will take place.[13]

However, while Latin America and Asia show trends well above the international average, the very poorest countries, including many in sub-Saharan Africa, do not show such rapid change.

- In 2010, just 6% of the population in Africa was over 60 years old, as compared to 22% in Europe overall.
- By 2050 the proportions will have risen to only 10% in Africa but 34% in Europe.
- In between, in Latin America and Asia, the over-60 population will have risen from around 10% to a remarkable 25% in the same period.

All of the population estimates for the UK, the EU and internationally are, of course, just estimates, which are continually being adjusted. They also mask differences that appear in particular countries. For example, in most countries there is an underlying preference for male children, but in some cases, for example in China, South Korea, Bangladesh, India and Pakistan, that preference impacts directly on the ratio of male children to females, which may be as high as 100 : 80.[14] In some countries young men's migration to seek work elsewhere affects the balance between the sexes, while HIV/AIDS has affected a generation in some African countries in particular, so that a higher-than-expected proportion of children are being brought up by grandparents rather than by parents.

In the Western world, we have talked about the huge increase in numbers of people who will live past the age of 85, and the vast increase in the number of those who might qualify to receive a card from the monarch in the UK when they reach their 100th birthday. However, we will not know for some time whether the impact of the change in life-style to one that is more sedentary, and the increase in obesity and consequent ill-health, will actually start to buck the trend towards a longer and longer life. But let us suppose that in general we will continue to be an ageing population, in which case the quality of that longer life is all-important.

Healthy life expectancy

The people we spoke to when writing this book, mainly in their 60s and 70s, with some in their 80s, overwhelmingly did not feel that they were old in the way that the media present an image of old people. Most of them were in good health, although wary about what the future might bring. Their attitude towards being old(er) was generally very positive, apart from concern about future deterioration in health. The question of healthy life expectancy is clearly vital for individuals and their families.

The WHO has developed a measure known as Health Adjusted Life Expectancy (HALE) so that we can measure not just how long people live but how long they live with a good quality of life.[15] In OECD (Organisation for Economic Co-operation and Development) countries life expectancy in 2001 ranged from 76.8 to 86.4 for females and 70.5 to 80.3 for males, but healthy life expectancy was on average 74 for women and 70 for men. It is likely that there will be some years towards the end of life when there may be some sort of limitation due to illness or injury. This, combined with the continuing growth in life expectancy and the ageing of the population, has tremendous policy implications for health and welfare. Older people tend to be generalised as needy and dependent, but, as we see in Chapter Six, many are working for longer, and generally they are as diverse as any other group in society. Inevitably there are those with major health problems, and we need to devote sufficient resources to health and social care to provide not just for the current generations of older people but also for those who will follow on. As we have already noted, the ageing of the population is continuing and is not a one-off issue. We look at both the provision of care and the economic implications of an ageing population later in the book.

Maintaining a longer healthy life not only is good for the individual but also makes economic sense for society. Policy implications associated with healthy life expectancy include the need to develop preventative approaches that stress maintaining fitness, the importance of a healthy diet and the need for social interaction (see Chapters Ten and Eleven). There are indications from research on ageing that at least some of the medical interventions and costs could be reduced. For example, research at Newcastle University has shown the tremendous impact that moderate exercise and a low-calorie diet can have on reversing Type 2 diabetes, as effectively as some major drugs,[16] and there are similar findings about dementia, where the estimates for future levels have recently been lowered as the impact of higher living standards and healthcare are taking effect.[17] We suggest that more effort and resources need to be given to the sort of research that will explore and develop interventions affecting life-style, helping to alleviate and prevent the sorts of long-term conditions that impact negatively on health towards the end of life.

Thinking differently about ageing

When we have a success story of longer life expectancy resulting from medical advances and rising living standards, why is the resulting ageing of the population seen in such negative and scaremongering terms?

The popular media make out that the changes are more acute in the UK, but in fact we are part of a global trend and our society is ageing more slowly than that in the rest of Europe.

We need to recognise that migration is a fact of life and that immigrants in search of better lives help to counter the trend of the population's ageing.

Of course an ageing population means that there are issues and challenges to face. There are many policy implications. We need more medical research on dementia and other diseases of the old, more of a stress on healthy living, a new look at social and healthcare, and innovative housing policies. We need to plan for a future where there will be so many more people in their 90s and over 100, and a greater proportion of older men.

What about the upside?

Living longer lives means that, as individuals, we can look at our lives differently, planning for career, family and community engagement over a longer, and hopefully healthier, life span. For many of us there will be an extended older age with opportunities to explore existing and fresh interests.

Families and society as a whole will benefit from the contributions of the increasing proportion of older people, as well as provide for their needs.

The way forward is not to fear or blame the old but to recognise the need to look afresh at ageing, and at our attitudes towards it. After all, none of us is immune to ageing and our aspirations should be to create an inclusive and caring society. Setting up structures and processes that support older people, and creating a climate of respect and care, will benefit not only the old people of today but those who will be old tomorrow.

THREE

How society ages people

"How old are you?" asked Joey from the nursery class. Caroline, one of the authors, was doing some research in his school.

"Are you very old?" he went on.

"Yes."

"Are you more than five?"

That encounter reminds us that how people see ageing is relative and that how we talk about ageing is learned from an early age and permeates many of our social interactions. Joey introduces us to some of the complexities of age and about what is considered old. In his school age was a frequent topic of conversation. For adults the pleasure to be found in the encounter with Joey comes from the dissonance between their idea of old and his. But for him, in a school where age and size mattered, it must have seemed a far-off aspiration to achieve more than five years. How people talk about age is learned through social interactions, and what is acceptable in talk about age varies across different phases of life and in different cultures and depends on who is doing the talking.

Language can disrupt dominant ideas by drawing attention to discriminatory practices and offering alternative perspectives. How we understand ageing is created through social practice, including language, so we can change perceptions through different use of language and social activities.

Common ways of talking about ageing and older people are examined in this chapter. We ask why people have the ideas and views about ageing that are current. What are the influences on the ways in which people understand and talk about ageing and older people? We look at where these views shape behaviour, responses and policy. We notice the restrictions and pitfalls in some of these discourses and arrive at some alternative ways of thinking, talking and acting that challenge dominant and unhelpful ideas and provide new directions for policy and individual action.

Influences on everyday narratives of ageing

Ageist assumptions are integrated into common discourse. We struggled with the language as we wrote this book. We wanted to avoid the terms by which our society communicates discriminatory attitudes about older people.

'Othering' is a practice that we wish to avoid. It implies that some people are not like us, as indicated by the use of the pronoun 'they'. Categorising people assists this process, as we can see in the use of the homogenising term 'boomers', which sets up generational opposition and feeds a desire to find 'scapegoats for collective social difficulties'.[1] Notions of decline and dependence are normalised through language. Many of the descriptive nouns in common use have pejorative overtones: wrinkly, crone, old bag, hag, old fart, bed blocker, coffin dodger. Undesirable behaviours and policies towards older people, cruel and unpleasant humour, resentment at perceived benefits, are legitimised through such terminology. Even terms like 'seniors' and 'the aged' have unwanted connotations for some. It can be argued that 'older' is a euphemism for 'old', but it is a more acceptable term. Other terms encourage the infantilising of older people through language: 'dear old thing' or 'our treasured seniors'.

We recognise the need for humanist researchers, including ourselves, to situate older people as 'co-equal members of society', to avoid 'both academic and social practices that stereotype, disregard or dismiss what goes on in later stages of the life course'.[2]

All representations of older people's experiences that 'stereotype, disregard or dismiss' need to be identified. We refer to these practices as ageism, a term first introduced in 1968 by Robert Butler in his description of the life of older people in America. He wrote in 1975:

> Ageism can be seen as a process of systematic stereotyping of and discrimination against people because they are old, just as racism and sexism accomplished this with skin color and gender. Old people are categorized as senile, rigid in thought and manner, old fashioned in morality and skills … Ageism allows the younger generation to see old people as different from themselves; thus they subtly cease to identify with their elders as human beings.[3]

Butler saw ageism manifested in a wide range of phenomena on both individual and institutional levels – in stereotypes and myths, outright disdain and dislike, simple avoidance of contact, and discriminatory practices in housing, employment and services of all kinds. He suggests that the strongest stereotypes relate to the '3 Ds' – disease, disability and death.[4]

Ageist attitudes still go unchallenged 40 years later. Society is slow to change and ageism is still not regarded on the same level as other 'isms' such as racism, sexism, heterosexism or able-bodyism. We do not accept sexist or racist insults, but older people are fair game for slurs, perhaps because the 'not-old' can distance themselves from the old.

Ageism can also be internalised when older people take on the social norms associated with youthfulness, such as covering grey hair or wrinkles, as we describe in Chapter Eight. Also, older people can deny having any link with others in their same age group. For example, the father of Eileen, one of the authors, when talking about taking out those 'dear old souls in their wheelchairs', was denying his age when in fact he was older than them. Toni Calasanti[5] points out that ageism includes 'age-blindness' – the belief that age doesn't really matter and that we should ignore age. We call this age denial.

Not all narratives of later life are ageist. A variety of theories have over time been developed to understand what happens in later life. Underneath all versions there are four influences at work, identified by social gerontologists, who study these things. For example:

- chronological
- physical
- psychological
- cultural or societal.[6]

Briefly, chronological ageing refers to the number of years one has lived. The people we interviewed mentioned physical evidence more frequently than anything else in understanding ageing. Ideas about decline and dependence as we age are strongly related to physical influences, and so are some beliefs about a responsibility to stay active. Psychological influences refer to individuals' feelings about ageing and the effects of those feelings on their behaviour. For example, some of our interviewees reported a changed sense of time, that there was less of it and that they needed to hurry up with their life projects. Cultural or societal influences affect how we talk about and behave towards older people, for example seeing decline as the defining feature of this time of life.

Dominant ideas about ageing and the old

Ageing and old people are frequently perceived and referred to as problems. In order to expose and challenge the narratives and language of ageism, we now explore the dominant narratives of ageing in our culture. We identify the outcomes of these discourses before introducing some alternative perspectives on the lifecourse and about age-inclusivity.

How are old are you, if you don't mind me asking?

Ageing and the number of years lived are closely associated, yet do not tell a consistent story. Chronological age provides markers of significant events in our lives – for example, starting school, getting the vote, being able to drive or to get married. And when we get older chronological age qualifies people for some advantages such as a state pension, a winter fuel allowance, travel passes, health checks and treatments, reduced admission to cultural events, a free TV licence. It can shift people into different categories, for example, a sportsperson's becoming a veteran at 50. It can make applying for some services more difficult, especially travel and car insurance, or giving blood. Bill Bytheway[7] points out that these days individuals' chronological ages have gained unprecedented salience through a concatenation of official documents, birthdays and time-related social expectations.

Acceptable talk about age depends on the generation of the participants. Young people are often asked to give information about their age. Joey inverted this when he spoke to Caroline. He and his classmates will learn that it is not polite to ask adults how old they are. Age becomes a taboo subject, except in humorous references to passing years in greetings cards. Big birthdays, when an individual moves from one decade to another, are celebrated as significant. In later life age reappears as a legitimate topic, often introduced by older people as part of establishing their identity: 'I'm 85 you know!' One study found that older people frequently referred to their age, either to explain something about themselves, such as, 'at our age we can't be expected to keep going all night', or to claim, 'I'm not doing too bad for 75. I can still walk up the stairs without getting short of breath.'[8]

Different rates of physical ageing are thought to be due to factors such as class, ethnicity and genetics, as well as life-style. The number of years lived may have little correspondence with how people feel. Some often find it hard to credit that they are their chronological age. Many of our interviewees echoed the comments of Robert, who said, "At 82 I feel like 55. At a younger age I thought 82 was past it!" And to ask people how old they are inside always brings a laughing response of usually a decade or more difference between their sense of self and their chronological age. We frequently subvert the idea of the significance of chronological age by referring to someone as '82 years young'.

Looking and behaving younger than one's actual years is celebrated in our culture. *Saga* magazine has a regular feature assessing the 'actual' age of famous individuals, gauged by assessing their activity and the extent to which they keep up with technological advances. They are always assessed as younger than their age in years. We note that there are many rules in general circulation about behaviour in relation to chronological age: women shouldn't wear jeans over the age of 50; women married to younger partners will find it hard to keep up; men are expected to be attracted to younger women; you can't teach an old dog new tricks.

Living one continuous life

The number of years may not matter very much to us as individuals, and later life doesn't necessarily represent a radical break with the past. Continuity theory claims that people age most successfully when they retain their habits, preferences, life-styles and relationships from mid into later life, when they continue to use their skills, coping strategies and learning to navigate any new challenges.[9] A person's characteristics and core values may become more pronounced with age: people who have always been active and sociable are unlikely to withdraw when older, for example. By replacing previous roles with similar ones, especially in retirement, people remain satisfied with their lives because there is consistency between current activities or life-style and previous ones. For example, professionals, like we three authors, who have published throughout their careers write about ageing. Most importantly, continuity theory counters the 'othering' of older people.

There are pitfalls associated with continuity theory, however. It does not explain the effects of social institutions, implying that people are immune to the dominant messages about ageing. It takes little account of chronic illness or changing circumstances. When Bryony (81) talked with us she suggested that it is not always possible to keep the same life-styles and relationships.

> "Friends can become infirm or die and particularly joint holidays may disappear.… It is also possible that we become less tolerant and more set in our ways and with not such an easy personality. Forming new relationships may be more difficult. There is also the economic aspect, life-styles cannot always be kept up."

Another problem with the idea of continuity into old age is that it ignores the powerful effects that learning and a sense of adventure can generate, such as ending work and going to live in France, or becoming a painter or poet. Rather than continuing as usual, some older people reinvent themselves and achieve innovative ways of living. Ageing can bring wisdom, rich appreciation of life, freedom of choice and time to develop important relationships, as we discuss later.

Seeing life as a series of stages

A different view of ageing is also widespread, focusing on stages in life. Because more people are living longer, commentators have recently, especially in the last 20 years, invented even more stages and categories to sub-divide older people. We are familiar with the idea of stages from Jacques' speech in *As You Like It*. He identifies seven stages in life. The final stage is unappealing, reflecting a deficit model:

> Last scene of all,
> That ends this strange eventful history,
> Is second childishness and mere oblivion,
> Sans eyes, sans teeth, sans taste, sans everything.

The categories of 'older old' and third- and fourth-agers have gained recent currency to differentiate healthy third-agers from dependent fourth-agers. Anne Karpf warns about the dangers of this approach:

> It doesn't take long to work out how dangerous this way of thinking is. We've created a new stereotype – that of the mobile, healthy and affluent 'new old', which at the same time demonizes the immobile, sick and poor 'old old'. It is as if old age these days only befalls those too powerless, poor

34

or stupid to do something about it. Those who shamefully surrender to the ageing process surely deserve what they get – 'unsuccessful ageing'.[10]

Karpf suggests that many people have a fear and loathing of ageing because of the notion of decline and dependency attached to being a fourth-ager, 'old old' or 'elderly'. People such as the former nurse Gill Pharaoh, whom we introduced at the start of the book, fear their own ageing if they associate it with requiring care and support.

Declining into dependence

The most widespread narrative of ageing is the story of decline. Physical decline was mentioned more frequently in our interviews than any other aspect of ageing, unwelcome because it is seen as inevitable and leading steadily to dependence. Amy (62) was typical, if brief, saying that ageing means "knowing that my physical and mental capacity will inevitably only decline". Ruth (64) said, "ageing is a reduction in physical health and it feels like there's nothing to be done about it". Elizabeth (89) made it clear that growing old was very unwelcome, referring to "the pernicious deterioration of the body".

Many of our interviewees noted particular limitations: being tired and weak, slower in actions, having less energy, more aches and pains, healing less quickly, failing eyesight and hearing, and incidents of forgetfulness and dodderiness. A largely undiscussed issue (a liberation to some, an unpleasant surprise to others) is loss of libido. Many saw their physical difficulties increasing in the future.

Christopher (67) described ageing in relation to an older generation:

"I feel middle-aged. I'm still working so I don't see myself as old and doddery. I've had some old relatives in their 80s and 90s. And I've known people of my own age who have died. Being old means being weaker, less able, especially physically and mentally. I don't look forward to that. I can see my own mother struggling with some of that. And ten years or so ago my father did too."

Amelia (64) made a similar point. She saw "real" old age in the light of her mother's situation: "I don't feel I am anywhere near real old age. At this stage I feel the twinges, but when I look at my mother I think my God, is that what is waiting for me. I hope I have at least 20 years before I get there."

Understanding ageing as a kind of systems failure is an idea that has been around for some time. August Weisman introduced the theory of Programmed Death in 1882, proposing that natural selection provides a specific death-mechanism to eliminate the old.[11] Ghosts of this theory are still around, especially in ideas of social and economic redundancy in old age.[12] In this narrative older people can be seen as weak, frail and incapable, and needing lots of care and resources – they are described as 'geriatrics' and 'inhabitants of God's waiting room'. Insulting images take the form of weary, worn-out creatures. Martin (72) said, "I hate that road sign of the bent old people with sticks."

The pitfall of this mechanical view of ageing is that older people become defined or define themselves by disintegrating bodies and minds. Such attitudes create a climate in which abuse occurs. Comedians exploit this dysfunction. One of the more offensive is the recurrent sketch of an older woman wetting herself in public week after week in *Little Britain*.[13] It is worrying that this programme appeals to younger viewers who come to accept these negative, so-called 'humorous', stereotypical images. The dominance of physical decline as the narrative of old age suggests that for many people this period of life is defined by the ultimate failure of the body – death. We found that much writing about old age, for example in fiction, focused on preparing for death, rather than on living and enjoying life.

Concepts of social redundancy justify exclusionary practices such as silencing, segregation and isolation.[14] The notion of economic redundancy also leads to discriminatory practices in the workplace, although these are illegal, and feeds exaggerated political claims about the growing burden of the dependent old upon the productive young, discussed fully in the next chapter on the economics of ageing. The assessment of people older than 65 as economically redundant is out of date.

Postponing the inevitable

A much livelier picture of ageing focuses on postponing old age and death through activity. In this view of ageing, physical and mental decline can be delayed, and the quality of life enhanced, when old people remain physically and socially active. This is the claim of activity theory.[15] Its influence is currently widespread. Many older people, including our interviewees, see activity as being the key to successful ageing. Many of them told us how they were engaged in challenging physical activities, such as Mike (70), a triathlete, and Ruth (64), who said:

> "I want to try new things and push myself, for example, I've just walked over the O2. This is about doing things I haven't done before and might have been scared of and then acknowledging it with a group of friends – new things like zip gliding. This might be about the prospect of mortality, doing things before I die – having adventures."

Of course, not every older person engaged in activity is trying to stave off decline. As Catherine (64) said to us, "many people stay active because they like doing things. It's not about trying to keep young, it's about enjoyment and about life now", not an insurance policy.

There are advantages in the activity approach. For example, public health policy encourages people of all ages to improve their health and well-being by walking and other physical and social activities. Such initiatives aim to keep people physically and socially active, increase employability and make participants as light a burden on society as possible.

Critics suggest that encouragement of one particular life-style, such as activity, is too narrow and is victim blaming: it is your fault if you get ill. Many older people do not have the health or resources to be active. Particular social factors, including poverty, rural residence, poor nutrition, substandard housing and limited educational opportunities can all reduce activity.[16]

The discovery of life-extending mutations to extend youthful appearance has transformed ageing research. Scientists have discovered that when single genes are changed animals remain young – physical changes occur more slowly. In humans, these mutants would be analogous to a 90-year-old who looks and feels 45. On this basis people talk about ageing as a disease that can be cured. 'The field of ageing is beginning to explode, because so many are so excited about the prospect of searching for – and finding – the causes of ageing.'[17]

Those wanting to postpone the ageing process may take advantage of other scientific breakthroughs. For example, Jane Fonda (77), when talking to Catherine Shoard, said she has returned to her acting career, having 'bought' ten years:

> "I have a fake hip, knee, thumb; more metal in
> me than a bionic woman.... I wish I was brave

> enough not to do plastic surgery but I think I
> have bought a decade ... the danger with surgery
> is you say: 'Oh this is good, let me do more'. It
> can be an addiction."[18]

A particular problem associated with the idea of buying years is that older people, women especially, are pressured into looking young. The use of Botox injections is normalised, and a vast cosmetic industry exploits older people in their attempts to 'defy' ageing, as we discuss in Chapter Eight. Cryogenics enthusiasts with money have taken this idea of a cure for ageing even further and have had their bodies frozen, in the expectation of future cures.

Stepping back

Old age, some believe, is a time for disengagement, to withdraw gradually from social and work relationships in preparation for the ultimate disengagement – death. Advocates of this view of the end of life suggest that it is a time to become preoccupied with one's own life and to accomplish specific tasks. The first is the acceptance of life, including what was accomplished and what was not fulfilled. The second is to achieve wisdom through undertaking this developmental task.[19]

Some of the people we spoke to referred to this idea. Lorna (59) said, "as I get closer to death and rounding off my life, I think it's become more important to reconcile things like my sense of self, my place within my family, my legacy and contribution". Joseph (66) told us:

> "Recently I decided that the need to think about
> my mortality was pressing. Time was becoming
> limited, energy itself becoming seriously depleted,
> and thoughts of actually changing the world

seemed now remote. The obvious strategy was to become more focused, in the scope of activities, in terms of choosing actions that had a greater chance of success, or which clearly need to be done. On the other hand it could mean a greater detachment from practical affairs and a concentration on psychological and spiritual factors."

In a practical way, Miriam (69) completed her family tree to pass on to her children and grandchildren, a process we describe in Chapter Thirteen.

Disengagement allows knowledge, responsibility, wealth and power to be transferred from the older generation, ensuring that younger people have jobs and roles. It is seen as beneficial to minimise the social disruption caused by a person's death, while allowing space and opportunities for younger people. Older people may want to disengage from their adult children, ensuring that they can function independently. As Miriam (69) said to us, "I feel I need to see less of my children. I don't want them to miss us too much." Aspects of this theory can be seen in political ideas about the duty of the older generation to provide materially for their offspring, the idea of generational contracts.

However, today many aspects of disengagement seem outdated, especially in cultures where older people are living longer and many are more confident in using technology to stay connected. Influences of this theory linger. Retirement is an illustration of disengagement, popularly seen as freeing older people from onerous occupations to pursue other activities, like gardening, golf and going on cruises. These images are ever present on retirement cards, often depicting retirees in rocking chairs. This view of retirement is increasingly out of date: many people continue working for longer, and others take up similar work, but unpaid, as they move into volunteering and community-support activities.

We see gradual segregation justified by disengagement theory in the gated communities that provide separate accommodation for older people. Eileen, one of the authors, visited pleasant retirement accommodation in Dorset, designed specifically for the over-65s although most residents were in their 80s. It had optional care and support services, adjacent nursing facilities and a care home; a church and cemetery were next door. Older people can slide seamlessly from independence to full-time care and then to their graves, with no disruption. The pitfalls in seeing older people from this perspective are that 'they' are no longer fit to engage in any useful occupation, just obsessed with themselves and their ailments, have no purpose in life and have nothing to offer to younger generations. Being old is an excuse to opt out or be opted out. Society is consequently deprived of a generation of talented, knowledgeable, inventive and wise people. Disengagement is an outdated concept.

For example, while some older people may start thinking about a time when they might require support in looking after themselves they are not disengaging from the world. In her book *Alive, Alive Oh!*, Diana Athill, now approaching 100, writes:[20]

> When one makes the difficult decision (and difficult it is) to retire from normal life, get rid of one's home and most of one's possessions, and move into such a place …, it means that one has reached the stage of thinking, 'How am I going to manage my increasing incompetence now that I'm so old? Who is going to look after me when I can no longer look after myself?'

While Athill is now living in a retirement home in Highgate, London, she is not disengaged from the world, and is writing wonderful books that give inspiration and joy to her many readers.

Acting your age

The idea that we learn to perform being old is illustrated nicely in this unsolicited Facebook message we received:

> Me and my partner are experimenting with being old for a few days ... he's had a hernia repair, I pulled a muscle in my hip the day before. Thanks to all friends helping out, especially for ferrying us about and getting the hot & cold patches! I think we'll survive! S'interesting the sorts of things that one might need to get 'a young person' in for eventually ... changing the bed linen for starters, that uses strength as well as stretch, even with a fitted sheet.

Jenny (67) is being ironic, knowing that this is a temporary situation, a rehearsal. But beneath this message speaks truth – an agreed cultural understanding of what it means to perform 'old' and how relationships with family, friends and younger people change as a result.

Some people fail to perform 'old' and are criticised by others who are influenced by dominant cultural ideas. Mike (70) told us that when he was preparing for a triathlon, friends said, "you must be mad at your age, you crazy man of excess. Why don't you just put your feet up?" Catherine (64) added that "an acquaintance of mine said she had not made a particular knitting pattern because the garment was too young for her. The mind boggles! And yet, there are some things I wouldn't wear now that I might have when I was younger." Bryony (81) said, "To do or not to do something physically challenging? The reaction of the coastguard and ambulance crew to a school friend of mine who fell on some rocks was one of reproach. The implication was that she should not have been doing that."

The stereotype of the grandmother carries a particularly strong picture of decrepitude, perhaps owing something to fairy stories, as Miriam (69) told us: "My grandson, aged six, mimes a bent old crone with a walking stick as an impersonation of a grandmother even though he has to deal with two extremely active ones." An alternative to the stereotype was featured in a woman's magazine celebrating three grandmothers, Eve Pollard, Edina Ronay and Joan Bakewell. 'Superficially it looks very much as if these three women are showing us that ageing is not a decline scenario, but reiterating that it can be IF one does not learn how to be a modern grandmother.'[21] Sadly, learning to be a modern grandmother requires conforming to a new oppression – the glamorous alternative to the old crone – when what is needed is a more realistic image of the grandmother to set alongside the traditional mythical version. Catherine (64) noted a general trend in our society, a feeling of obligation to stay young and for society to limit the options or ranges of how it is OK to be.

Young people learn to perform differently with older people, for example by addressing them in ways that infantilise. "People call you dear and then treat you as if you are an idiot", said the actor Dudley Sutton, aged 82.[22] His story is featured later in Chapter Fourteen. Different forms used by care workers in addressing older people also illustrate this point, a theme we develop in Chapter Ten.

Generational conflict over resources

Dominant beliefs shape policy. For example, beliefs about older people's dependency are reinforced by reference to state pensions as benefits, on a par with unemployment or sickness benefits. This can be compounded by referring to older people as pensioners, when their economic status may be irrelevant. An example is of a man who had to fly a plane when the pilot died at the controls. His pensioner status was irrelevant, but reference to it implied less competence than 'retired business man', and so made a more edgy story. Martin (72) felt that this kind of language was unhelpful. Interviewed by us soon after the 2015 general election, he said:

> "The political discussion is rubbish. It's not helped by the misleading idea that pensions are benefits. It prevents discussion moving forward. It is not a benefit when you have contributed to National Insurance all your working life on the understanding that you can draw a pension when you retire. It is an entitlement based on a social contract."

Policy makers face difficult questions. The perceived relationship between ageing and the economic structure frames how they deal with these issues. Since the state decides the allocation of resources, the social worth of older people is determined by these decisions and in turn shapes prevailing attitudes: any discussion about change in the welfare state reinforces the stereotype of the burdensome elderly.[23]

An interesting dynamic emerges: governments might choose to reduce resources, such as limiting pensions, but in doing do would risk alienating the older electorate. Political parties are careful not to alienate older people, as a greater proportion of them tend to vote.

One political discourse blames older people for scarce resources, and stokes fears about the perceived increasing burden of dependency. We see this in David Willetts' book *The pinch: How the baby boomers took their children's future*,[24] further discussed in Chapter Four. Younger people are encouraged to think that all older people (the boomers) have done too well, live in expensive houses and are getting in the way, taking the money, jobs and houses that rightfully belong to the young. This is misleading about both the older and younger generations.

Blaming the boomers ignores the productive roles that older people fulfil, such as volunteering, childcare and looking after older members of the family. But even this can be distorted if it is seen as a duty – and as a justification of reducing public expenditure. Grandparents are expected to look after their grandchildren. If they don't conform, they are considered selfish.

What can we take from these different views of ageing?

The most common ways of perceiving ageing and older people are inherited and out of date, as they take little account of the increased longevity enjoyed by so many more people. More seriously, they encourage exclusionary and discriminatory practices. Framing lives in terms of ultimate frailty and death can deny people the opportunities of the present. And this response to increasingly complex life on our planet, of seeking scapegoats, is depressing and ageist. We must not create a new ageism in response to demographic changes.[25]

What needs to change?

There are different stories to tell – those of celebration, with the darker side of ageing not denied but also not dominant. We need to share stories of ageing that avoid separating older people from others or suggesting that people are no longer recognisable in the last years of life.

We need to promote the lifecourse perspective, rather than other theories, as it presents a more accurate and general picture. This perspective sees ageing within a lifelong process and takes account of the diversity of roles that change across the life span. Development is viewed as occurring throughout life, not as limited to certain stages.[26] This perspective offers a multidisciplinary approach, drawing on history, sociology, demography, developmental psychology, biology and economics for the study of people's lives, structural contexts and social change. It focuses on the powerful connection between people and their historical and socioeconomic contexts. This perspective avoids the linguistic features of the dominant stories of decline and dependency relating to the latter stage of life.

Importantly, this perspective takes account of the gains and losses that occur throughout life. Events and roles are not expected to proceed in a given sequence, but make up the sum of a person's experience. Development is considered multidirectional, with stability or development in some areas and decline in others. Just to take one example, ageing may lead to impairment in short-term memory but not in creativity or social function. With this perspective in mind, it would be easier to notice and challenge ageism.

Alternative understandings of age and ageing need to be promoted:

- ageing is not a story of steady decline, not a series of stages, but fluid;
- the later years are not dominated by death, but part of a rounded life;
- older people are not a separate category, not 'them' but 'us';
- older people do not come from one generation, but several generations;
- older people are not responsible for society's problems, but valuable assets.

We need to hear the multiple stories of ageing, characterised by diversity of income, health, sexuality, ethnicity, marital status and other variables.

We need inclusive and integrated attitudes, not exclusionary and discriminatory practices.

We need to reclaim alternative representations of ageing so as to prevent erroneous and damaging ageist practices. The following chapters present such alternatives.

FOUR

Time bombs and agequakes: the economics of ageing

It is excellent news: more people are living longer! What's more, they are living longer in good health. But this good news is often drowned out by misconceptions and scaremongering about the economic consequences. In Chapter Two we set the record straight about why the population is ageing and how this is affecting, albeit in different ways, every part of the world.

We went on, in the next chapter, to assert that perceptions of age and ageing are culturally influenced and have changed over time. We suggested that current ideas about ageing have not caught up with research and lived experiences. For example, the idea of relentless decline in old age is a very strong one, and it reinforces the idea that expensive care will be necessary for longer. Yet the HALE statistics, quoted in Chapter Two, indicate that people are living longer with a good quality of life.

Building on these ideas, this chapter challenges the scaremongering talk of an impending economic catastrophe, arguing instead for preparation for the changes. We point out that there are political choices to be made about social and economic responses, noting that the short-termism of domestic politics discourages longer-term plans.

We argue that there are political reasons for orchestrating doubts about the capacity and willingness of our society to care for an increased number of older people, and for hiding other truths about the causes of and solutions for wider economic problems. It is easier to blame people than to face up to challenges. It also encourages ageist and derogatory attitudes and implies justification for discriminatory practices.

The scary story

The raw figures do indeed suggest that we are in for trouble. Two sets of figures are used to evaluate the burden of the ageing population: the absolute figures on the number of people alive, and the proportions of older versus younger people. Both sets of statistics have implications for society, but it is the proportional figure that is most used to justify the idea of catastrophe.

The age pyramids in Chapter Two show the population's changing age structure. The base of the pyramid, the younger generation, is shrinking, which leads to rectangularisation of the population structure. This shrinking reinforces the impression of instability.

Population figures related to age are relevant because a society has to support its dependent people through the economic activity of its working population. This is most frequently expressed as a ratio between the number of people over 65 and those of working age. It's called the old-age dependency ratio or age-dependency ratio. The simplistic version of this ratio is both misleading and frightening, as it suggests that the moment is very near when the burden of financial dependency of the old will be too great for the young to carry. This is the argument for the time bomb. The catastrophe prediction has been around for 35 or so years, since the 1980s, and it has not yet materialised. So perhaps we should take a closer look at what is happening.

Unpicking the scare stories

The age-dependency ratio

The age-dependency ratio requires close scrutiny, for it is crude and misleading. The crudeness in the calculation is a function of the assumptions upon which the calculation is made.

The age-dependency ratio is expressed as a percentage. Today there are 310 people of pensionable age for every 1,000 of working age and therefore the old-age dependency ratio is 31%. It is expected to rise to 37% in 2035, even allowing for planned rises in the State Pension Age (SPA) to 68. How bad is that? Should we be worried by a ratio of 37%, or even of 31%? Where is the breaking point?

Age is a poor predictor of dependency, and the critical word here *is* dependency. But to simplify the calculation, the most-quoted ratio does use age as an indicator of dependency. It sets those over the SPA against the working-age population. Using age as a proxy for dependency inevitably calculates that as the population ages a greater economic burden will fall upon younger people.

To assume that economic dependency starts at the age of 65 flies in the face of reality. The evidence is everywhere. Many people over 65 continue in employment. About 3.5% of the total workforce is over 65 and the proportion is increasing. Since the abolition of the Default Retirement Age DRA in 2011 people have been able to choose to continue in work until they are ready to leave. We should not be surprised by the willingness to work among a group whose health has been improving. Further, some older people need to continue in work for financial reasons. We explore the need and willingness to work longer in more depth in Chapter Six.

The word 'dependency' conjures up ideas of poverty and benefits. However, over-65s continue to make substantial contributions in many ways. Those still in paid employment continue to pay income tax, and about five million over-65s are paying income tax on their pensions and other income. Even those who have left the workforce, or who reduce their hours, frequently have increased spending power, as compared to previous generations. The spending power of the over-65s, the 'grey pound', is itself a major contribution to the national economy and, as we argue in the next chapter, is frequently overlooked by those who could benefit from better attention to older consumers.

Many older people make a substantial contribution of their time and money to charities and to the care of family members, reducing the costs for both the state and the family. Nearly two million grandparents have given up a job, reduced their working hours or taken time off work in order to look after grandchildren. Grandparents make substantial financial sacrifices as well: 12% have spent over £1,000 on their grandchildren and 3% say that they have reduced the amount they have saved for a pension in the previous year, in order to support their grandchildren, according to a poll for Grandparents Plus in 2014.[1]

The other side of the ratio also needs re-examining – the people of working age who have to support the dependent old. The ratio as it is usually given relies upon the assumption that everyone aged between 16 and 64 is economically productive, and fails to take account of those who are unable to work due to disability, lack of employment opportunities or unpaid care responsibilities. In fact there are more dependants of working age (9.5 million) than there are older people who are not employed. A truer picture of the dependency ratio would use the number of people in employment, including the one million over-60s.

Economic productivity, rather than age, provides a more meaningful and accurate calculation, allowing us to see that dependency has actually fallen by one third since 1976, and in the future may stabilise, probably at about 29% in 2050. It also indicates that at no point will it reach the levels experienced for most of the twentieth century. In the last three decades of the twentieth century the figure was 30%.[2] The care of dependent members of society is a matter of competing political choices, discussed below. However, inaccuracy, scaremongering and exaggeration are not the best basis for discussion of the challenges to be met.

The numbers

A second set of statistics to fuel the concept of a time bomb or agequake are the numbers themselves. More people are living longer. The argument of impending catastrophe rests on the assumption that because they are living longer they will need care for longer. For the population as a whole, however, the periods of chronic dependency will continue to occur in the final years of life; that is, dependency will be delayed, not increased. The WHO's measure, known as HALE, reveals that most people aged 65 in the Western world can expect to have about nine more years in good health. While healthy life expectancy is not rising quite as fast as life expectancy, the prediction of catastrophe relies on the argument that the increased number of older people puts unsustainable strain on health and social care provision.

'We should not assume that population ageing itself will strain health and social care systems,' warn the authors of an article in the *British Medical Journal* (*BMJ*), 'Population ageing: The timebomb that isn't?'.[3] They argue that most acute medical care costs occur in the final months of life, and that the age at which these months occur has little relationship to numerical age. The figure for dependency of older people would be more accurate if based on remaining life expectancy.

Will there be an inevitable crisis?

The scare story implies the inevitability of an explosion, and also responses to the challenges of the ageing population. But there are choices to be made at every level: by policy makers, local communities, families and the individual.

The increase in the older population is widely presented as problematic. During the winter of 2014–15 the news frequently contained items about a hospital crisis in acute care. We learned that beds were being 'blocked' – that is, that no appropriate provision had been made for people who were fit to leave hospital but still needed care. This is a crisis of funding, of priorities and a function of the lack of coordination of healthcare and social care for older people. But in this version of the time-bomb story older people are perceived to be causing the crisis in public expenditure by 'absorbing more than their fair share of tax-payers' money', to quote the bishop of London.[4]

The emphasis on state provision for older people is especially pernicious when it is contained within ideas about intergenerational fairness. There is a perception that older people are being protected, especially their pensions and age-linked benefits such as winter fuel allowance and bus passes. It is assumed that governments seek electoral advantage by favouring the older voters, who are known to exercise their right to vote in greater proportion than younger people. Whatever the electoral advantages, there are good reasons to continue to support the old and not simply to transfer benefits to the younger generation.

- Older people have contributed throughout their working lives to their pensions, and it is more accurate to refer to the state pension as an entitlement than as a benefit.
- Older people deserve care, support and respect for their lifelong contribution.
- It is cheaper to provide some benefits in the short term than to pay for the more expensive consequences later. For example, there are benefits to free public transport in preventing isolation and loneliness, as well as enabling access to healthcare and other services. It is both more humane and more efficient to prevent loneliness and poor health than to deal with chronic but preventable conditions.
- Many older people are already suffering from the austerity cuts and are still among the poorest in our society. They would be badly affected by any removal of benefits.
- Economic analysis suggests that transferring public spending from the old to the young would 'have very little impact on intergenerational inequalities and the long term prospects of younger cohorts'.[5] To put it another way, the answer to these problems isn't to make older people worse off. The benefits provided for older people come to younger people in the future.
- Other policy options than denting the older generation are available to improve the economic outlook for younger people.

Because there are greater inequalities between classes or income groups than between generations, it is a distraction to frame the economic policy choice as one of supporting the young at the expense of the old, or vice versa.

So, there are social changes and economic challenges as a result of ageing for longer, but the story of the time bomb is an exaggeration. The scare stories are based on age rather than dependency, and fail to take account of increased healthiness in old age. Since the start of this century, academic research has challenged the Doomsday scenario.[6] We now turn to consider the reasons for the persistence of the idea of the time bomb.

An explanation for the repetition of the time-bomb story

The idea that the increase in the older population is a time bomb can be shown to be exaggerated and a distortion. Who is promoting the idea of a fearful future, and why? The media as well as politicians are accused of operating in an 'evidence-free zone' by Professor Alan Walker, the leader of the biggest social research project, the New Dynamics of Ageing.[7] A consequence of the 'evidence-free rhetoric' is that it allows distorted versions of the challenges and causes, including the idea of the time bomb, to gain traction in public discussion.

In whose interest is it to perpetuate the idea of an impending crisis?

- It makes good headlines.
- It diverts blame and criticism by obscuring some of the effects of recent policies.
- It dodges serious economic analysis.
- It diverts attention from the inequalities in our country that still leave many older people in extreme want (although fewer than before).
- It favours short-term blaming over long-term planning, which suits election-conscious politicians with an eye to the next election.

Above all, it feeds the prominent discourse that blames older people for the difficulties of the younger generation. We have lost count of headlines that begin 'Boomers to blame for …', including increased rudeness in society, shortage of hospital beds, difficulties in getting decent jobs or promotion, and student loans. You can add any social problems to this list. The discourse is not limited to politicians.

> Our parents had free education, fat pensions, early retirement and second homes. We've been left with student debt and a property ladder with rotten rungs. And the only career choice is a crap job or no job. Thanks very much. (Andrew Hankinson)

This comment comes from an article about a 'lost generation' in the *Observer Magazine* in January 2010. The article laid the cause of the younger generation's difficulties at the door of the older generation. Selfish and greedy are frequent descriptions of the spoiled so-called 'boomer' generation.

We should note the sense of entitlement of the younger generation, and that some commentators have gone as far as claiming that an established social contract between generations has been broken because the old have held on to their wealth. This new ageism reflects a shift away from the idea that the old, dependent population is deserving of our care and interest, and toward a feeling of entitlement by the young to the wealth of the older generation.[8]

These arguments that blame the older generations were advanced in 2010 by Conservative MP David Willetts in his book *The pinch: How the baby boomers took their children's future – and why they should give it back* – a clever title, implying both a financial squeeze and theft.[9] The premise of his argument is that an intergenerational contract has been broken. Others have contributed to this idea of the entitled younger generation, for example *Jilted generation: How Britain has bankrupt its youth*.[10] Culprits can quickly be identified: people born between 1945 and 1965, the 'boomers'.

The rational approach to an impending crisis is to make plans to mitigate its worst features, not to stand on the side-lines and throw blame. All this talk of intergenerational conflict and projection of a crisis waiting to happen is a diversion from necessary action.

However, we should acknowledge that some government policies are already shifting to encourage people to work for longer, and that changes are under way that are intended to improve and coordinate social and medical care in local communities.

A different story about the economics of ageing today

Although the media often present the spectre of a time bomb, informed citizens are not convinced. When we spoke to Richard (70), who had had a career as an international corporate banker, he told us about his suspicions of talk about time bombs. At a public event Caroline, one of the authors, was gently upbraided by a GP for her intemperate talk about a looming crisis in care for the elderly. He referred her to the *BMJ* article mentioned above that questions the time bomb scenario.[11]

Professor Sir John Hills, professor of social policy at the London School of Economics, spoke at an event at the Royal Academy in February 2014 about the burden or benefit of the ageing society. He suggested revised titles for the books mentioned above.

> The pinch: How *some of* the baby-boomers took *other people's* children's future – and why they should give it back *to more of them, not just their own.*

> Jilted generation: How Britain has bankrupt *some of* its youth, *but others will be OK.*

Thomas Piketty, the French economist, has made a detailed and long-term study of sources of capital and wealth in *Capital in the twenty-first century*.[12] He traces the changes in wealth over the last century, and from this we can draw some interesting trends.

First, social class remains more significant than generational differences.

> To be sure, older individuals are certainly richer on average than younger ones. But the concentration of wealth is actually nearly as great within each age cohort as it is for the population as a whole. In other words, and contrary to a widespread belief, intergenerational warfare has not replaced class warfare. (pp 243–4)

Wealth inequality exists, but it is not a function of generations. Piketty's analysis concludes that inequalities were reduced, or 'compressed', as a result of two world wars and the Great Depression of the 1930s, and with a little help from progressive taxation, but that over the last 25 years they have been increasing again.

Second, Piketty reveals that inherited wealth is not being squandered by greedy so-called boomers, although it is contributing to the increasing inequalities in wealth. Again, this contradicts the claims of those who promote the idea of generational conflict. In 1880, 24% of wealth was inherited. By the 1950s this had decreased to 4%. It has now risen again to 14%. These figures are from France, but it is likely that the British figures follow the same pattern. Piketty states:

> Inheritance is playing a larger part in their [younger people's] lives, careers and individual and family choices than it did with the baby boomers. (p 381)

Given that people are living for longer, the older generation need to provide for themselves for longer. The so-called boomer generation received less in inheritance than the generations before or since, but need to hold on to their wealth for longer before passing it on at death. It is ill-judged to criticise those who make provision for more years in retirement.

That is not the end of this part of the story. The average age at inheritance has risen from 30 years to 50 years and you might think that this explains the discomfort of the younger generation. The older generation may have delayed some of the inheritance they give to their offspring by dying later, but they have increased the amount that they transfer to their offspring during their lifetime, and to such an extent that Piketty calls it 'a golden age of gift-giving' (p 393). The average age for receiving this bounty from living parents is 35–40 years, and for the most part it is in the context of real estate (property) investment. And when the younger generation do finally receive their inheritance it is larger than it would have been 20 years previously, because capital tends to reproduce itself and accumulate over time.

We see the evidence of intergenerational assistance all around us, and not just in inheritable wealth. Two-thirds of first-time house-buyers get financial help from their parents, according to the Council of Mortgage Lenders. And parents help in other ways. Three million younger people are staying at home for longer, unable to afford to buy a property for themselves (an increase of 20% since 1997). We have also already noted that many older people provide care and financial support for their grandchildren. Referring to the poll about grandparents, Bobby Duffy of Ipsos Mori said,

> The survey illustrates very clearly that the idea of there being a 'war' between the generations is very far from the day-to-day reality for most people. In

fact, it's the opposite – it shows how many young families rely heavily on grandparents for support.[13]

The myths of intergenerational conflict and the time bomb are promoted for political purposes. They drown out the reporting of the beneficial economic effects for our country of the increased number and proportion of older people. These are happening now.

> Older people already make a disproportionately large contribution to the Big Society. As a group they do more than their fair share of volunteering, charitable giving, voting and other forms of civic engagement, from petitioning to becoming councillors.... The fact that older people already volunteer, vote, donate and engage in the community more than other age groups is itself a route to further progress.[14]

This is taken from a report that suggests that older people will continue to play a significant part in the resolution of our economic difficulties. And this while the proportion of GDP (Gross Domestic Product) spent on social care is much lower than in other European countries. The UK's expenditure was 6.1% in 2012, compared to Austria's 12%, Sweden's 9.4% or Denmark's 8.4%, and among the lowest in Europe.[15]

What needs to change?

Public debate about the economic consequences of increased longevity needs to be much better informed. There are economic costs to the ageing society, but just as rabbits are startled in the headlights, people's responses are frozen by the domination of the catastrophic scenario. The debate has become polarised as the old are blamed, or considered favoured, or people feel helpless.

More knowledge will provide better discussion and dialogue and lead to better policy. Our book is intended to help with this de-obfuscation. Politicians and the press, in particular, need to become more familiar with the research and to promote more research. And we could benefit from looking at what is being done in response to the challenges in other countries throughout the world.

Economic discussion that is based on age categories should be challenged. The older generation includes such a diversity of people, especially in terms of wealth, that age categories are frequently irrelevant. Such categories also mask inequalities, especially in income and wealth.

We need to challenge the out-of-date story of doom and gloom. In its place we need to tell a different story. This one would celebrate what the active older generation are contributing to society: increased economic activity through their employment, payment of taxes, care provision, charity work and their buying power. This different story would explain that older people are holding on to their wealth (if they have it) for longer because they need to, but that they are also giving more during their lifetime to their offspring. Indeed, the generation who benefited least from inherited wealth (the so-called boomers) are giving more to the next generation than they received. Talk of greed and blame should stop.

Planning needs to replace blaming, especially in political discourse.

Planning for the implications of an ageing population needs to be long term. At the moment, arguments for planning are obscured by talk about intergenerational conflict.

Long-term policy planning is difficult in the face of political time, where an election is always less than five years away. Planning for social changes needs to look ahead further than five years. This is also true at local community level, especially where health, social care and accommodation are concerned.

Alternative solutions to the social problems of inequality need to be given wider consideration; for example, taxing assets more, looking again at what people give away tax free to their offspring or looking at equity gains from property.

Individuals need to plan for a longer life, with longer time in employment as well as in retirement.

Providing for a longer life makes sense. So does talking less about an impending and inevitable crisis, and doing more to prepare for the problems and opportunities that we can expect from increased longevity.

FIVE

Overlooked and under-estimated: older consumers

A quarter of consumers in the UK are aged over 65, yet 90% of marketing expenditure is targeted at the age group under 50. The over-65s are an increasing market sector, forecast to grow by 81% by 2030, in contrast to the younger market (under 50s), which will grow by only 7%. There are few signs, however, that these statistics are having an impact on advertising. For example, why do you never see an advertisement for a top-of-the-range car featuring a driver over 50, when 80% of purchasers are over 50?

The failure to take account of the growing older market leads us to conclude that older consumers are overlooked and under-estimated. Why does it matter? It matters because older consumers are not well served, their needs are ignored and they suffer poor product design. Furthermore, advertising reflects the ageism that we identified in Chapter Three, by ignoring older people except where age-related products are identified, as symbolised by the Stannah stair lift. In this chapter we consider the consequences of five enduring myths about older consumers and argue that categorising the population according to age serves neither consumers nor producers well, as it ignores the factors that influence consumer behaviours.

And it matters, because the growing wealth of older people, the so-called grey pound, is potentially very valuable to the economic life of the country.

The previous chapter rejected the claims for Doomsday scenarios as the consequence of increased longevity. Here the story is one of neglect and failure to capitalise on the potential benefits of the changing market. It does a disservice to everyone.

Older consumers

The spending power of the over-50s is rising three times as fast as that of any other group, and they account for 40% of consumer demand in the UK. It makes little business sense to target the group without money and ignore those with it. But this is what frequently happens. A director of market research whom we spoke to acknowledged this. "We need to shift perceptions. Everyone wants to target the younger generations although the money is with the older generation!" And more directly, later in the interview she observed, "this audience is the one that is growing, but it is not sexy to advertisers".

The following are some significant features of the older consumers.

- The spending power of the over-65s is one of the most important aspects of the market-place.
- This spending power is large and is growing as the population ages.
- People over 65 are as diverse as any other age group and there is no commercial advantage in treating them as a homogeneous group.

- Consumer behaviour is changing among the 65+ age group, as with everyone else.
- Advertisers frequently define older consumers in out-of-date terms, or neglect them except to promote age-related products.

Older consumers are a growing group and their tastes are also changing, as Stefano Hatfield observes:

> But, what most of the advertising industry, in particular, and the media generally have failed to notice is that today's 50 is not our parents' 50. We are not only blessed with greater life expectancy (currently 79 for men and 82 for women), but are healthier, wealthier, more energetic, and entrepreneurial than any previous similar age group.[1]

Here is a description of current 60-something consumers, reported in the *Independent* in 2011:

> [They are] happier than their younger counterparts, feeling financially more secure and physically more robust. They take more holidays than any other age group; nearly half take two or three trips abroad a year. Perhaps surprisingly, they have also been embracing technology (email, Skype, Facebook and internet shopping) with age appropriate enthusiasm.[2]

Note the word 'surprisingly' in the last sentence of this quotation. It assumes a connection between ageing and technophobia, which is discussed below. We should not be surprised that 'older people want good products and services in the same way anyone else does'.[3] Older people buy soap powder, party food, white goods, cars, DIY products and smartphones, just like everyone else.

Research into the changing needs and behaviour patterns of older consumers is lacking, perhaps because those in the business believe they know about them already. This lack of evidence-based knowledge is a 'market failure', according to ActiveAge.[4] Businesses are missing opportunities by accepting and reproducing myths about the interests of older consumers and not taking account of the different ways in which the current older generations are spending their money. It seems that many marketers don't know that they don't know, or believe they can thrive without updating their knowledge. The failure to take account of changes in older consumers' spending is not new, but has been around for half a century, according to a research review for Age UK called *The golden economy*.[5]

Advertising and the media have a very close relationship. The omission of older people from the media (explored more fully in Chapter Seven) makes it less surprising that advertising largely ignores older consumers. Unless products are considered appropriate to their age, older consumers are ignored. Richard (70), who had worked in the trade, confirmed this. "On the one side the target is Stannah stair lifts and walk-in baths, the other side is that you are invisible as an older person."

Myths, stereotypes and invisibility work together to homogenise the image of older people and hide the inequalities that persist in British society. Nearly a million people of pension age (900,000) live in absolute poverty, and this has been increasing (by 100,000 between 2010 and 2014). Black and ethnic minority pensioners are more likely than white pensioners to be living in poverty. The most at-risk group are Asian pensioners, according to Age UK.[6] So, while this age group as a whole should command more attention, the diversity, including considerable poverty, within the age group also needs recognition.

Consumers who have difficulties with eyesight, physical flexibility, mobility or transport are also poorly served. It has been shown that changes that would be effective to improve their consumer experiences are often minor and involve such things as lighting, the height of shopping trolleys and packaging.

The grey pound is a significant but overlooked feature of economic life. It is growing and changing. It is also diverse. Marketing approaches miss commercial opportunities and, by relying on a narrow range of outdated beliefs, perpetuate stereotypes.

The myths about older consumers

Consumers of all ages are changing rapidly, but failure to keep market intelligence up to date means that redundant stereotypes of over-65s persist, and determine product marketing. ActiveAge suggests that a great deal needs to be done to shift attitudes in the market-place and to displace ageist thinking.[7]

Segmenting the market so as to identify different groups provides the basis for product development and product promotion. The oldest consumers are segmented by age, and failure to research means that manufacturers and marketing people retain inaccurate information. Marketing is especially culpable here, but it also affects product development and design, packaging, instructions – the whole consumer experience. The five myths about older consumers, adapted from Stroud and Walker's *Marketing to the ageing consumer*, underpin most marketing and product development.[8]

Brand loyalty

The first and very powerful myth is that older consumers don't change their choice of brands. They are not seen as discerning or informed consumers. One implication of this is that there is little point in targeting them with information about new brands or changes from which they might benefit. However, research into older markets shows that 70% of people over 50 think that their viewpoints have changed since they were younger, and 50% want to learn new skills and become involved in new activities.[9]

Older people's habits don't change

The second myth is that older people's purchasing habits extend beyond brand loyalty: for example, they change their car every four years, or always use the same supermarket for a weekly shop. No doubt this is true for some older people. But not for others. Businesses will miss out by not communicating to adventurous older people.

It's all about the young!

The third myth is that the most lucrative market is youth. The statistics quoted at the start of this chapter suggest that this is no longer the case, especially for expensive items such as housing or luxury cars. Furthermore, it is believed that a strategy that targets older people will alienate the younger market, so that the fear of product association with older customers keeps older people in the background of marketing campaigns. But there is no evidence that the young are put off by age-friendly or age-inclusive campaigns.

They are included anyway

Another assumption is that marketing material reaches older people anyway, even if it is designed for a younger market. This argument makes no sense in, for example, the luxury car market. Why pitch a campaign at younger buyers who are less able to afford the product and when 80% of the purchasers are older customers? Do advertisers believe that older people want to be seen as young and sexy, so they will buy a product associated with sexy youth? Perhaps it is assumed that older people share the stereotypes and do not want to be sold products by older people.

Older people are technophobes

In the early years of e-mail and the internet older people may have been less familiar with new technologies. But personal computers, smartphones and tablets have been around for some time now. Many who are in their late 60s used computers in their professional lives, have younger family members to assist them if necessary and want to learn because of the opportunities for accessing information and communicating easily with others. Already in 2012, 50% of over-50s believed that technology had made life easier and 70% had used the internet to purchase goods. The most-consulted source of information for holiday bookings in this age group was the internet.[10] Age is not the most significant determinant of internet use. These are nationality, education and socioeconomic groupings. The misconception of technophobia is shared beyond the world of commerce, as indicated by the word 'surprisingly' in the above quotation from the *Independent* about 60-something consumers embracing technology.

Marketing practices draw upon a composite image of the older consumer who is set in their ways, not interested in new products, avoids new technologies and needs no attention unless they want stair lifts and walk-in baths. And because the beliefs about older consumers are persistent and shared, little market research is being undertaken.

The exclusion of older consumers

The consequences of the myths are that product development and design, retail experiences and advertising are excluding many older consumers.

This matters for people whose dexterity and vision are adversely affected, because their difficulties are ignored in product development and design. This is an area where small changes can have a big effect. Inclusive design would avoid difficulties for consumers and promote product sales.

Take the example of electronic gadgets. Amy (62), recently retired from a career in IT, referred to this failure of design in her interview:

> "I feel that electronics now can provide amazing gadgets that could help elderly people enormously. Some things such as mobility scooters have provided great help to people. However, other gadgets such as hearing aids and other things that could be really helpful are sometimes not as helpful as they could be, because they work technically but are not designed around ease of use for those who may have either reduced physical capability or reduced capacity to learn how to use new things, or maybe both."

The design of mobile phones is a particular source of dissatisfaction.[11] Telecoms firms focus on persuading people to change contracts, but ignore the features of the phone itself, which was a particular complaint highlighted by the *Independent*:

> The buttons on many phones are so small, they're hard to use – and they haven't brought phones to the market that deal with such issues. In fact, they have gone to extreme lengths to make things even smaller rather than to be legible, not just the buttons, but the menu options too.[12]

Another example of failure, this time in marketing strategies,[13] concerns a remote-control device by Sky TV that was designed with visual and dexterity impairments in mind. It had larger and bolder graphics, raised, contoured buttons and increased contrast between the buttons and the body of the device. It was recognised for its excellence. It would have appealed to many people, not only older consumers. However, it failed to sell initially because the company had not considered how potential customers would find out about it. It didn't appear on the Sky TV website and Sky's own call-centre staff didn't know about it. The company has now put the device on its website.

Access to the point of sale, whether in shops or online, is the most significant factor in a person's buying activities. Transport plays a major part in older consumers' shopping habits. Rural consumers without cars are the most excluded, as public transport is so limited. Some big retailers, such as M&S, have had success with providing dedicated transport to their store. Small changes to improve consumers' access to online shopping include better-designed websites and online support. Within shops, changes to the lighting, trolley heights, print sizes on packages, as well as simplicity of packaging and assisted shopping, have all been shown to make shopping more accessible for people with reduced physical capacities.[14]

Older people have a wider range of interests, needs, activities and demand for products than is suggested by the myths. According to the report *Silver cities*,

> When people think of the silver consumer, they immediately think of the obvious sectors – healthcare, pharmaceuticals and adapting homes for independent living. However, older people constitute large proportions of consumers in many other broad sectors, particularly leisure and tourism, financial services, consumer goods, food and beverages, retail and technology. Households with a head of household aged between 50 and 64 spend more on both health and recreation than any other age category.[15]

Over-50s in the UK buy, for instance, 50% of skincare products and 80% of leisure cruises and of top-of-the-range cars.[15]

In magazines targeted at older people you discover what advertisers think appeals to the over-50s. Some very small-scale research into the advertisements in one issue of *Saga* magazine (excluding only the many adverts by Saga's own companies for travel, insurance, financial services and so on) revealed the following spread of products in order of frequency:

- retirement homes (11)
- mobility aids (6)
- bathroom adaptations (6)
- home extensions (6)
- chair and bed reclining adaptations (5)
- home lifts (5)
- new kitchens (4)

- vitamins (3)
- food-delivery services (2).

A relatively high number of adverts for home extensions and new kitchens might be found in any general-interest leisure magazine. These items are not age specific, although savvy marketers will be aware that people in this age group often have disposable income to spend on their homes.

We can see that the targeted, Stannah stair lift and walk-in bath approach is alive and well. These products are also not age specific, even if the market for them is assumed to be. We all know people of different ages who have benefited from products aimed at older people. A friend with mobility problems had a stair lift fitted when she was in her 40s. A mobility scooter has enhanced the life of a friend in her 50s, still in full-time work, who has restricted walking capacity.

The manner in which age-targeted advertising is pitched can be alienating and offensive, as Bernadette (66) observed in her interview:

> "Daytime TV, which I am studying for a research project, makes me feel sick. The adverts particularly are patronising, focused on ill-health and immobility, and dying. The one featuring Ronnie Corbett having meals delivered to his door, with the jolly repartee, makes me want to spit. The ones for stair lifts, and walk-in baths are just as bad, especially the one where an older woman is seen flirting with a young delivery boy, much to her husband's annoyance."

The targeted approach can also be an exploitative one. Beliefs that ageing is a series of problems – of ill-health, immobility and dying – for which solutions can be purchased lead to exploitation. Age-targeted marketing can encourage consumers to invest in a solution they don't need or want. The exploitative stance uses the fears and problems of old age to promote products. Some fears are well founded, but others are orchestrated for profit. Who is making money out of ageing? What fears are exploited? We have noticed the following in the last few years.

- Anxiety about crime promotes separate and gated communities and security devices, despite falling crime statistics.
- Fears of Alzheimer's disease promote the sale of electronic gadgets, despite the evidence suggesting that such devices represent a reductionist view of keeping mentally active and make little difference.
- Mis-selling of financial services and products, and encouragement of equity-release schemes exploit financial fears or ignorance. *Choice* magazine warns about the new freedoms to take a full pension pot at retirement, noting a threefold increase in scams since their introduction.[16]
- Potency anxiety, especially for men, resulted in the development and sale of Viagra.
- Fears about appearances and ageing have spawned the cosmetic industry's anti-ageing products and surgical procedures (see Chapter Eight for a full discussion).

Fears are fed by the frail and dependent images of older people. It is widely believed that the older population is most at risk from street crime, while the statistics show that it is actually the 20–30 age group who are the most at risk and that crime is falling. The fall in crime could be reassuring to older people, but fears about safety and crime feed the demand for gated communities and security devices. *The Guardian* in 2011 reported a case where rogue traders had frightened their elderly victims into buying ineffective and expensive security systems.[17] Their marketing material featured 'the gloved hand of a burglar opening a window, a ransacked room, a shadowy figure standing outside a house', in order to sell burglar alarms. Customers spent £6,000 for a 15-year contract. The company has since closed.

Marketing practices focus on age, despite other factors being more significant in consumers' behaviour: nationality, gender, health, education and employment status all influence buying behaviour more than age does. To base marketing strategies on outdated myths about older consumers does not make commercial sense.

A range of possible approaches to older consumers

Alternative approaches to marketing can vary from the most excluding to the most inclusive. We explore the effects of each approach, to consider how each serves older consumers.

Neutral approach

Older people are not happy with marketing approaches that ignore them. They do not see themselves in adverts, except in those for targeted products. Stefano Hatfield, also quoted above, wrote this about turning 50:

> I'm waiting for advertisers to talk to me; target me
> in a look and tone that is aspirational. It looks like
> being a long wait, even though by 2020, 50% of
> the population will be over the age of 50, and we
> already control 79% of UK disposable wealth.[18]

In her interview, Juliet, also recently turned 50, told us that she felt that 50 is "the disappearing age" in advertising and the media generally.

> "It seems in all the advertising that 50 is the cut-off
> period, the age at which you are classed as 'old' ...
> once you get to 50 there are household and car
> insurance policies where the premium is reduced
> due to your age and of course you can always go
> on a Saga holiday!"

She went on to complain that older people are not often
represented as stylish dressers or energetic grandparents.

These impressions are confirmed by a market research
director who noted some recognition of the under-70s, but
she repeated one of the myths about older consumers being
stuck in their ways when we spoke to her.

> "From an advertising perspective we don't directly
> talk about this age group. They are very different
> in terms of attitude and life-style to younger
> audiences. We can segment the over-70s but they
> tend to be more fixed in their attitudes."

Age-friendly approach

Some companies have tried to widen the appeal of their
products by using older celebrities in their advertising. For
example, Helen Mirren was used by Nintendo to front the
Wii Fit Plus campaign of Christmas 2011; Joanna Lumley
was used in the Müller Vitality campaign; Keith Richards
promoted Vuitton luggage in 2008 and Twiggy has been one
of the faces of Marks & Spencer (M&S) clothes since 2005.

Developing friendlier product designs is another way of
becoming more age friendly, as in the example of the Sky TV
remote described above. Sky's failure to promote it indicates
that the company still needs to ask potential customers about
their purchasing practices. A more inclusive approach to the
age group would mean that older people would be present

in advertising campaigns, in the background, in a crowd, as a friend, as the informed person, as the expert, for example.

Writing at the end of the 20th century about the focus on age segmentation, Andrew Blaikie reported the slow pace at which market researchers were changing:

> Yet for all the sophistication of psychographic segmentation, lifestyle analysis, and other forms of detailed niche marketing, the bottom line in selling to the old seems to be age itself.[19]

He pointed out something we still see today, that is, how fond researchers were of segmenting people by age-decades:

> under-65s ('primelifers') are distinguished from people over sixty-five ('seniors'), the 'young old' from the 'oldest old', the 1900–10 cohort from the 1910–20 cohort on the basis of mindsets attaching to the key 'time signatures' of each decade.

Amy, the former IT specialist, referred to this in her interview:

> "People over 60 are old people, who are treated as a generic group, as though when we turn 60 we suddenly stop being individual human beings. They also forget that over-60s now include two or three generations."

Blaikie also looked forward to the day when advertisers will break the taboo on old age. It still seems a long way off.

Age-inclusive approach

The age-inclusive approach goes beyond the age-friendly and does not focus on age, but on the potential value of the products or services to consumers. Two existing examples of product development and marketing illustrate this approach.

First are the Good Grips products, which were developed for people with dexterity problems, but are well designed and appeal to everyone.

Second, the myth of the old as technophobes is busted by the success of Apple, and especially its iPad tablet. The sales approach is consumer friendly, with outlets on the high street, clear information, products displayed at waist height, a sales force of all ages. Access is not an issue in purchasing the goods. As for the product, the interface with Apple's icons has always appealed to geeks and non-geeks alike, and to people of all ages.

Consumer power: the new factor

The spending power of older consumers is growing. And while companies may at the moment be slow to appreciate the implications of these changes, they will increasingly know about them. The generation moving into their 60s and 70s have always been outspoken and are increasingly competent in the digital technologies. They will favour the age-inclusive and the age-friendly. There are plenty of patronising attitudes out there that this feisty generation will get stuck into. They will not suffer being stereotyped by companies, or ignored by them. And more, they have the purchasing power to make a difference.

We can already identify some shifts in design and marketing approaches as a result of consumer power, as the examples of Apple and Good Grips demonstrate. Other campaigns that are frequently put forward as evidence of change are Dove products and M&S clothes for women. Diane Kenwood, editor of *Woman's Weekly*, told us about the pressure that eventually forced a change to the M&S Classic range.

"I'll give you an example of how things are changing. For a long time older women have wanted dresses with sleeves and finally M&S are listening and producing fashionable clothes with sleeves, not just constraining them to the frankly, still disappointingly dowdy, Classics range, but in their fashion ranges as well. And it's not as if this is a new example of older women wanting fashionable, flattering clothes. While I was working on the magazine, M&S launched the Per Una range, which was aimed at 18–34-year-olds. They were astounded when they discovered women who were buying this range were actually 55–70."

What needs to change?

The argument for age-inclusiveness is pragmatic, in part. Inclusion of older consumers in marketing practices has the potential to bring their growing wealth to the economic life of the country.

The myths persist. While marketing to this sector is defined by age, the stronger influences of class, education, ethnicity and gender are underplayed.

Moving away from the dominance of age segmentation has the potential to improve product development and design.

It avoids the idea that the old are a homogenous group, recognising the many variations in age, outlook, aspirations, health and so forth.

An age-inclusive approach would not allow offensive images such as the short-sighted dodderers who cannot tell the difference between a roller-coaster and a cheese sandwich.

SIX

Working longer together

People are living longer and in better health. As a result more people are staying in work for longer. But older workers are criticised for taking jobs from the young. At the same time they are criticised for the growing costs of pensions. They can't get it right: they should not stay in work and they should not draw their pensions. As we have noted in previous chapters, older people are often blamed for the consequences of increased longevity.

In addition, older workers are frequently subject to ageist attitudes and practices. There are three main issues:

- getting the older unemployed back into work;
- lack of flexibility in working conditions to make working longer more appealing;
- ageism experienced in the job market and in employment.

Because the number and proportion of older people are growing, and because it is government policy to encourage people to stay in work for longer, these issues and challenges have become more sharply felt. We are frustrated when the debate is not based on up-to-date information – for example, about the value of the older worker to employers, to the country's economy and to the individuals who continue to work. Rather, there is a time lag that results in the persistence of ageist practices, such as resistance to employing older unemployed workers, and failure to offer training.

More older workers

Many of the people we spoke to as we researched this book welcomed retirement because it brought increased freedom. Some said they were looking forward to not working full time, increased leisure, freedom to do what they liked with the day. Others saw the end of work as the onset of old age. Christopher (68) said, "I feel middle-aged. I'm still working so I don't see myself as old and doddery.... Old age means stopping working, a physical decline."

Boundaries between work and retiring are eroding. Most women have worked all the time, not always in paid work, and continue to make an economic contribution through their domestic labours. Voluntary work is increasingly common among older people. Voluntary work both in the charity sector and in unpaid care makes a valuable economic contribution.

There is already a trend for more people to stay in paid work for longer. In June 2015 1,166,000 people aged over 65 were in employment, according to official statistics.[1] This number included a rise of 60,000 in six months, and the rise is a continuing trend. Between 1993 and 2011 the number of people entitled to a state pension who remain in employment doubled to 1.4 million.[2]

Government policy has encouraged staying in work for longer through the abolition of the DRA and raising of the SPA. Some people choose to remain in work for financial reasons. Many older workers need to top up their occupational pensions through additional contributions, perhaps because they have had periods out of work or have taken part-time work, resulting in lower contributions. Women fall disproportionately into this category, often having taken time out to care for the family, worked part time and not been available for promotions until later in their working life.

Financial reasons, especially pension prospects, mean that some older people need to continue in work. Nineteen per cent of men and 37% of women aged between 55 and 64 have no private pension investment and will have to rely on state pensions.[3] Others will want to build up their contributions so as to make decent provision.

It has been calculated that another million people would consider continuing in work for longer if the conditions were right, such as adjusted hours or adapted duties.[4]

Some people enjoy their work and see no reason to leave it. They may want to continue the social contacts with friends that they have made through work and enjoy being part of a mixed-age community. Margaret (71), a retired teacher, reflected on what she had lost when she left work:

> "I am not mixing with young people any more and I had enjoyed working alongside them. Those with families may not notice this but others can feel they have been separated from a wider society."

Work often provides structure to a person's day and a reason to get out of bed in the morning. Continuing in work can be important to a person's sense of purpose and usefulness.

Wise employers welcome older workers, whose skills and experience add to the resources of the workforce. Unfortunately not all employers are sympathetic, and older people in work frequently report that they are not offered training and promotion opportunities. Still others report leaving work before they wanted to because the conditions of their work no longer suited them.

Employers need to remove obstacles and encourage older workers to stay in the workplace. This involves action in three areas: removing ageist practices, providing flexibility in working arrangements and assisting preparations for retirement.

Tackling ageism

Age discrimination 'is deeply embedded in the culture, policies and practices of many organisations', according to the Equality and Human Rights Commission report into employers' attitudes.[5] The Chartered Institute of Personnel and Development (CIPD) noted that many managers apparently resist change:[6]

> Many older people are keen to carry on working or to embark on new careers but they often face obstacles caused by stereotyping, inflexibility or simple lack of imagination about how work could be organised differently.

The older workforce has changed: it is more educated, more skilled and less likely to be affected by health problems than ever before.[7] There is a significant time lag on the part of employers in ensuring that recruitment processes and workplace arrangements are adapted to these changes.

Tackling ageist attitudes is important for business. Guidance from the Trades Union Congress (TUC) and CIPD in *Managing age* states:

> Age discrimination is bad for business because it causes an unnecessary waste of talent, skills, knowledge and experience as well as undermining social cohesion and personal achievement.[8]

Practising discrimination on account of age is unlawful, but it happens. The discrimination can take the form of failure to recruit, to promote, to retrain or to provide adjustments in working conditions. These failures result from a set of beliefs that need to be challenged. They reflect the cultural idea of decline, especially decline in physical and cognitive abilities, as a result of ageing. The evidence suggests that there is no foundation to this belief to justify ageist practices. A review of research into age and employment concludes:

> There is little evidence that chronological age is a strong determinant of health, cognitive or physical abilities, sickness absence, work-related injuries or productivity.[9]

Deterioration in performance in work is not linked to increased age, for three reasons, the research found. First, 'most jobs do not require employees to work at full capacity'; second, functional decline can usually be compensated for by the worker's strategies, skills and experience; and third, variability in functional capabilities between individuals is very large and not associated with age. On the other hand, older workers are associated with some qualities that are valuable to employers: good time keeping, helping co-workers, better anger management and people skills.

Training and retraining are often not offered to older workers, on the assumption that it is a wasted investment. The truth is that it makes good business sense to achieve the best-quality workforce and be up to the minute in training. Training younger workers results in them taking their skills elsewhere, whereas older workers are more loyal to their employers.[10]

Employers appear to believe the old saying that you can't teach an old dog new tricks. In fact, older workers have frequently indicated in surveys that they want to continue updating their skills and that many would welcome promotion. One example is the unpredicted uptake of apprenticeships by older workers, the so-called silver apprentices. In November 2011 it was revealed that 400 over-60s signed up to apprenticeships in 2009–10, and 3,910 signed up the following year, out of a total of 163,000 apprenticeships. The picture is of resourceful older workers, demonstrating a willingness either to retrain or even to receive training for the first time.

The picture for many older women workers is worse. More women are employed than in previous times. They are working longer as their SPA rises to equalise with men's. They are still paid less than men, which affects both their current financial situation and their pension prospects. Many work part time. About 50% of women workers aged between 50 and 64 are in the public sector, and therefore particularly affected by public sector cuts. Many have zero-hours contracts or work for agencies and therefore their employment is precarious and less protected. More women take on caring responsibilities in addition to their paid work. They suffer more low pay, less job security and receive less training.[11]

Flexible working arrangements

Inflexible approaches to working practices are the biggest challenge to older workers. Flexible arrangements encourage their retention. The examples that follow are all successfully operating somewhere in the UK. Usually, this kind of flexibility requires only small adjustments, not major reorganisations.

Flexible hours

The most obvious and most attractive form of flexibility is in hours of work, allowing older employees to fit in other responsibilities, such as caring for older or younger relatives, volunteering and their own interests. In 2014 the UK government extended the right to request flexible working arrangements to all employees.

The most common form of flexibility is part-time work. The combination of some income and some disposable time can be very positive for older workers. A recruitment campaign for bus drivers in Brisbane, Australia specifically targeted retired workers with a campaign that featured combining the job with activities such as golf and spending time with grandchildren. Unpredictable demands placed upon workers in their roles as carers can be met through flexi-time.

Another flexibility is the gradual reduction in hours towards retirement, in one or more stages. In most countries, workers phase into retirement through reduction in hours and this is becoming more common in the UK. A smooth transition from employment to retirement can benefit both employer and employee.

Flexible working location

For those who can work remotely, flexibility of workplace location can be very advantageous, perhaps meaning that less time spent on travel. It can also benefit people with caring responsibilities or with some form of disability, or who want to fit in work alongside other activities.

Bridging jobs

The bridging job is specifically designed for older workers who still have much to offer, but not necessarily by continuing in the same post. It can be a bridge into retirement, offering modified physical demands, or can include new responsibilities such as mentoring less-experienced workers.

Re-employment

Many older workers move in and out of work following 'retirement'. Academic staff at universities, for example, may continue to work as researchers or student supervisors. Someone with particular skills can provide cover when the substantive post-holder is on leave, or off sick. Offering skills as a self-employed consultant can also work for both employer and older worker. A fee-paid arrangement can provide both sides with advantages: the employer benefits from the experience and skills of the former employee and the employee can work flexibly, with more control over their hours. The needs of temporary or part-time workers should not be neglected: desk space, access to computers, administrative support and being linked into communications about workplace developments.

It has been the case that public sector organisations have been significantly more likely to offer flexible working than the private sector. This may be less possible as austerity bites further into the public sector. Flexible arrangements are in the main available only to more skilled workers, who are already well placed in the job market.

Job sharing

Job sharing has long been popular with women with care responsibilities. The arrangements offer the possibility of working part time in a high-quality job. For older workers and their employers another attraction of job sharing is the opportunity to work alongside a younger worker and to guide and teach them, a kind of mentoring or coaching role.

One big company that has developed a range of flexible practices is BT, where 32% of the workforce is over 50. The head of BT's diversity practice wanted to accommodate the needs of the grandparenting community. *Managing age* reports that BT's encouragements to stay in employment include:

- wind down (part-time or job-share posts)
- step down (reduced responsibilities)
- time out (sabbatical)
- helping hand (charity or community work)
- ease down (reducing hours in the 12 months prior to retirement).[12]

Employers have a duty to make 'reasonable adjustments' to help workers with disabilities to remain in work (Equalities Act 2010). For some, it may be appropriate to reduce the burdens or responsibilities, sometimes called downshifting. Others may require a change in work arrangements. For example, for those with cardiovascular and respiratory decline, modifications might include changes in work design or use of equipment for lifting, restricting heavy physical tasks or increasing the number of breaks. A nurse who is no longer able to lift patients, for example, but who still has many skills that are needed in the NHS might have such modifications made to their responsibilities. Managers can introduce other modifications appropriate for workers with declining sensory function, such as hearing, or musculoskeletal function. Sympathetic approaches to psychological conditions such as depression can also enable people to remain in work. The benefits of such modifications are not restricted to older workers, of course.

Despite some good practice, many employers are currently losing key talent from their organisations by failing to offer flexibility in the workplace.[13] In evidence to the House of Lords, the CIPD claimed that 76% of older workers reported that employers had not made any reasonable adjustments in response to requests to help them continue in work. In contrast, a high percentage of employers reported the beneficial effects of offering flexible working arrangements on staff retention (75%), motivation (73%) and engagement (72%). Employees report better work/life balance and management of child and elder care, according to the CIPD.[14]

Preparation for leaving the workplace

Even if the over-60s are delaying their exit from the workforce, all will leave eventually. A good employer demonstrates commitment to the needs of their workforce by investing in the well-being of employees approaching the end of their career just as they do in the induction of new staff. The decision about the date of retirement, the ability to take time over this decision, the need for knowledge about pensions and life after work – all these can be assisted by the employer.

Good practice includes the following:

- a well-publicised retirement policy;
- the provision of information, especially about pensions;
- the provision of support for making decisions, through seminars and workshops, coaching and mentoring;
- ensuring a good farewell.

An effective retirement policy includes information about the purpose of the policy itself, the actions and practices that are expected of managers and retirees and the entitlement of the employees to the rituals of leaving.

A poor understanding of pension entitlements is unfortunately very common among employees. A third of employees 'do not even have a rough idea of what their pensions may pay out', the National Association of Pension Funds calculated in 2012.[15] Its research showed that lack of knowledge might be a barrier to workers' continuing in employment. For example, 40% of the people asked said that they would consider delaying their retirement if they could defer their state pension in return for higher payments; 59% were unaware that this option already exists. And again, 42% said they would consider delaying their retirement if they could combine income from their occupational pension and their current job; 60% were unaware that this is already available to many employees.

Briefing sessions on pensions and pension choices can help people to plan the financial aspects of retirement more efficiently. Access to, or information about, sources of professional financial advice for individuals is also very valuable. Workshops or seminars that encourage participants to consider the transitions of retirement can help to prepare them for other aspects of life. These can be provided in-house or in courses from dedicated providers.

Hannah (54) was a district nurse before she took early retirement. In her interview she told us:

> "Maybe there ought to be a bit more helping people to prepare for retirement and to stress the importance of being active. People seem to look forward to retiring but you could have 30 years of retirement, potentially longer than you might have worked. Maybe what should happen is a more phased entry into retirement. If companies would provide opportunities to be more flexible, a more phased retirement might help people."

A key event is likely to be the retirement party. For many it is a ritual that provides an opportunity for goodbyes, thank-yous, tributes and the acknowledgement of all that an individual has contributed to the organisation and their field throughout their career. Not everyone will want such an event, but every organisation can offer to plan it with the retiree, and to contribute to its success. The memory of how one's working life ended can stay forever and colour one's attitude towards the next phase of life.

Older unemployed workers

A missing million workers are the over-50s who are out of work, according to a report published in 2015.[16] The media tend to concentrate on the problem of youth unemployment, which indicates that attitudes towards older workers are out of step with economic trends and needs.

Statistics indicate that workers in this age group who are unemployed for longer than 12 months rarely make it back into the workforce.[17] In June 2015, 126,000 people were in that position, more than 40% of the unemployed in the 50+ age group. The comparable proportion was 36% for people aged 25–49. Unemployment among the older age group has increased, despite the overall figures falling. Many women have suffered, as they are not well protected: they are more likely to work part time, with agencies or in zero-hours contracts and in jobs vulnerable to public sector cuts.[18] The figures hide personal hardship. Many of these older unemployed people have not yet reached SPA.

There is an economic and business argument for tackling the problem of the older unemployed. The changing composition of the population means that there is already a significant demand for older workers to work for longer. By 2022, 14.5 million jobs will be opened up through people leaving the workforce, but only 7 million younger people will be entering the workforce.[19] In addition to the need for more skilled workers, the valuable skills and experience of older workers are being lost from the workforce when older workers cannot get jobs.

Ageism in recruitment is a serious barrier for the older unemployed, as well as being illegal. But it happens. The following research was recorded in the report *Too much to lose* for the Policy Exchange group.[20]

> We applied for over 1200 jobs as both an older and younger worker, using a randomisation process that ensured the CVs received by potential employers were identical in every way apart from the date of birth. We then measured the number of responses that showed an interest in the applicant.
>
> The responses showed a very large bias against older workers, with the 51 year old applicant getting positive responses less than half as often as the 25 year old. These results are similar to results from other studies that also find biases against older workers in some positions. It is startling to see that this discrimination happens even though the UK has very clear laws designed to prevent it (primarily the Equalities Act 2010) and it suggests that there is a culture of bias against older workers.

The same beliefs about older employees work against the recruitment of older people: fears about the capacity of older workers to change, or to fulfil commitments. Clearly, those responsible for recruitment need to address recruitment issues. Baroness Altmann, Minister for Pensions, was Champion for Older Workers in the 2010–15 Coalition government. At that time she suggested the following actions to human resources departments:

- more age-inclusive material in advertisements;
- a focus on experience as well as qualifications in the selection process;
- apprentice schemes for older workers;
- setting targets and age monitoring of recruitment to help identify progress.[21]

While there is support for people trying to get back into work, it has been criticised for being mainly aimed at younger unemployed workers and it has been suggested that JobCentre Plus advice should be more flexibly tailored to older workers.[22] For example, some need training in IT skills, especially as a quarter of jobs are advertised exclusively online and about two-thirds of employers state that e-mail and word-processing skills are essential.[23]

Are older workers taking jobs from the young?

Old beliefs are difficult to shift, even among older people, so the belief persists that older workers are taking jobs from younger people. Yet, as reported in the previous section, statistics indicate that in the future the numbers of younger people will not match the available jobs.

There is a persistent belief that there are only so many jobs to go around. In the past this has been repeated as an argument to keep women out of the workplace. Now it is used against immigrants and older people. 'They're taking our jobs!' Economists call it the 'lump of labour' theory. Sinclair quoted from *The Economist* (2011) to explain the fallacy:[24]

> [It] was once used to argue that women should stay at home and leave all the jobs for breadwinning males. Now lump-of-labourites say that keeping the old at work would deprive the young of

employment. The idea that society can become more prosperous by paying more of its citizens to be idle is clearly nonsensical. On that reasoning, if retirement age comes down to 25 we would all be rich as Croesus.

The truth is that a skills gap is looming, and in some industries is already upon us, especially in industries that currently rely on older workers: for example, in manufacturing, education and healthcare. This is what Kevin Green, chief executive of the Recruitment and Employment Confederation, said in June 2015:

> There is an enormous skills crisis looming. The UK is suffering from skills shortages across the economy and at the same time businesses say they can't take on more work without more staff. Older workers have a huge amount of experience, skill and knowledge to offer organisations. To encourage older people to stay in the labour market employers need to be more effective at attracting and retaining older workers. That's why we are so passionate about working with Age UK on this important initiative.
>
> Simple things like changes to the language used in job descriptions and where roles are advertised could be significant. We want hirers to work alongside specialist recruiters who understand the benefits that older workers can bring, and who can help tailor job roles to meet their needs. Together we can rid the labour market of out-dated prejudice and create a fairer and more productive economy.[21]

What needs to change?

Britain needs older workers, and many people need or want to work for longer. But the persistence of ageist attitudes discourages older workers from staying or applying for work. Businesses are losing out as well, as vital skills, knowledge and productive workers are lost to them. We need better-informed managers so as to ensure that exclusionary practices and attitudes are eradicated.

In Chapter Four it was suggested that dependence by older people is exaggerated when age is used as a proxy for dependence. People are making an economic contribution by working longer, and also through voluntary and unpaid work. This needs to be acknowledged in the statistics and in the debate.

As working life changes, boundaries between work and retirement are eroding, especially among older workers. Most women have worked all their adult life, not always in paid work, and increasingly make an economic contribution through their employment as well as their domestic labours. Voluntary work is increasingly common among older people. Pensions and retirement are less synchronous. The disappearance of a defined moment of leaving work indicates the changing picture of employment for older workers.

SEVEN

Media exclusion

> This is how it's done. Not just to me, but routinely
> when they decide it's time for you to go. They
> starve you of work – then point out your low
> productivity and the fights you've had to get your
> reports on air. Now you're not just unproductive,
> you're also difficult. I decided to leave quietly,
> without a fuss. Just like so many others. Only
> Miriam O'Reilly – braver than the rest – had
> fought the enormously powerful BBC and won.[1]

Olenka Frenkiel, an ex-BBC reporter, was writing here about
her own experience of seeing older women gradually being
excluded from key roles in the media. Although older men as
well as older women are not always so visible in the media, it
seems that older women in particular are disproportionately
absent from the visual media, from our screens, from
newspapers and magazines, and also from the ranks of those
who commission and produce TV programmes, films and
advertisements. The ageism of the job market, explored in
the previous chapter, is commonly experienced by those
who work in the media, but in addition the way in which

older people are generally presented in the media works to reinforce stereotypical images of older age.

In this chapter we focus first on the way in which stock, narrow stereotypes of older people tend to dominate in the visual media, despite the reality that the population of older people is actually enormously diverse. We then focus on the particular absence of older women from the media before, finally, drawing on our interviews to answer the question 'Are things changing?' and to envisage an alternative relationship between the media and older people.

Stereotypes of older people in the media

Representation of older people in the media tends to be relatively sparse, and where the old are represented, most coverage relies on stereotypes of age as weak and dependent. In the visual media such as newspapers and magazines, older people are often represented by stock figures, showing old age in a negative way that is certainly unrecognised by most of our interviewees. Juliet, who is in her late 50s, summed it up:

> "they are always depicted in old-fashioned clothing and needing stair lifts and although there are, unfortunately, many older people who suffer with ill-health and disability there are a lot of older people who are now looking after grandchildren (which takes a lot of energy), who are doing exciting things and going to exciting places, having interesting and fulfilling jobs and who dress in modern clothes befitting their age. I think maybe there is too much ageism … older people need better PR."

Janet (85) felt particularly strongly not just about the visual representation of older people but about how their importance to society is portrayed:

> "I react with anger and outrage. It's appalling. I don't see me in what they say. I'm an independent OAP [old age pensioner] as are lots of people of my age. There are very narrow media stereotypes especially on TV and radio: stereotypes of highly dependent pensioners. It is not credible that you have a brain, that you feel important and significant, that you may still be fit. It [the media stereotype] doesn't fit most people I know and people I work with, retired people."

There is something of an obsession with youthful beauty in the media. Anne Karpf refers to 'the denigration of age [which] is built on the idealization of youth', stating that both representations are far from the realities of life.[2] Although the most common stereotype of older people presented in the media is one of dependence, there is another, less prevalent but also untypical; that is of the glamorous exceptions. Don (72) identified this image as "elegant models who happen to have white hair". Talking about both stereotypes, he went on to say, "I don't relate to either of these images, nor does anyone I know". He felt that "real older people are invisible in the media because they are not perceived to be interesting", and while older people are regarded as 'other' and many of those working in the media are very young this may well be the case.

Some of those working in the media recognise these two stereotypes of older people, and that it is the second type, the glamorous exceptions, that make it onto magazine covers. Catherine Westwood, editor of the women's magazine *Essentials*, told us, "there are the exceptions. Helen Mirren is the face of L'Oréal, Charlotte Rampling of NARS". She went on to point out how untypical they actually are:

> "Older women can look amazing. Mary Berry looks marvellous. People will think 'I can look like that when I am 80'. But famous older women are actually living a privileged, rarefied life-style that is not typical of regular pensioners."

When asked if these exceptions simply proved the rule, Diane Kenwood, editor of *Woman's Weekly*, took a positive view: "these people make the rules change. You need a high profile for that." At least this view of the older woman is a positive representation in the media, even if the same few glamorous women crop up time after time, with standards of appearance that are unrealistic for the vast majority.

The stereotypes of older people that are used in the media ignore the incredible diversity of the old, including not one, but a number of generations. Like the rest of the population, the old, however defined, have an enormous range of socioeconomic circumstances and conduct their lives in a multitude of ways. Overall, older people are not well represented in the visual media, but in a society with increasing ethnic diversity, the absence of older members of ethnic minorities is particularly marked. When older people are featured they tend to be white and middle class. Talking about images of older people in advertisements, Bernadette (66) stated:

> "Who dreams up these images of how older people spend their time and the sorts of relationships they have? It is horrifying. There are no black people represented, no gay men or lesbians. I suppose I should be pleased about that, as imagine what

nonsense would be dreamed up to represent their
lives."

Age appears to be an attribute that crowds out all other aspects
of diversity, with images of older people in advertisements
and in the media tending to be relatively homogeneous,
mainly dowdy and traditional, with the few glamorous
exceptions who belie their years; but the people in the images
are almost always white, middle class and heterosexual.

Older women in the media

Invisibility as a form of social exclusion is experienced by both
men and women, but is experienced in a more intense form
by women, as ageism is augmented by misogyny, affecting
both their employment and their visual representation in
the media. Older men are often seen as distinguished and
wise and valued for their experience, although occasionally
mocked for an inappropriate comb-over. But there are
some brutal stereotypes and depictions of older women, as
we will see in the next chapter. Women in general tend to
be represented by an unrealistically slim and glamorised
image that is hard to emulate for the young and impossible
for the old, while the very term 'old woman' can be used as
an insult in our culture.[3] Older women may quite literally
feel invisible, having the strange experience of simply not
being seen, of people bumping into them or looking through
them, their eyes seeking out someone younger and therefore
more important. There is a scene in Doris Lessing's book
The summer before the dark where the main character, who is
in her 50s and on the cusp between mature attractiveness
and older age, walks down a road dressed first as an older,
then as a younger woman.[4] As she passes some workmen,
the reactions she gets are in complete contrast. They wolf
whistle and shout to her when she is her 'younger' self and

completely ignore her as if she is invisible when she is her 'older' self.

As pointed out at the start of the chapter, older women have particularly poor access to positions of power in the media, for example, BBC reporter Olenka Frenkiel writing about the subtle ways in which women are eased out and then prevented from discussing why they had to leave their job. The Older Women's Commission in the UK revealed that 82% of TV presenters over the age of 50 are men.[5] It seems that once women presenters reach the age of 50 the majority are side-lined or find that their position is no longer tolerable. Mariella Frostrup reported: 'I shed half my workload the moment 50 appeared on my CV'.[6] The Older Women's Commission reported that in the UK only 7% of the total TV workforce were women over 50, including both those on and off the screen. Research commissioned by the BBC in 2011 that aimed to inform the media industry about how the audience regarded age portrayal and representation revealed that a major concern was the lack of coverage on television of older people, particularly women.[7] Men tend to dominate in all areas of film making, with a five to one ratio of men to women across the industry, and 91% of directors being men.[8] If women are rare, older women are even rarer, and an initiative financed by Meryl Streep has been established to encourage women screenwriters in TV and film who are over 40.[9]

Women in politics face many difficulties, as compared to their male colleagues, but older women in politics face a particular brand of ageism–with–misogyny. It is unlikely that comments about Hillary Clinton such as 'I don't know how far they can pull back her face' and, if she were president, 'Will this country want to actually watch a woman get older before their eyes on a daily basis?' would ever be made about a man of a similar age.[10]

Are things changing? Different ways of being old

> Our collective mental image of what 30, 40, 50
> years old looks like lags far behind the facts ... if
> I read about a 70 year old grandmother, I don't
> think of my mother – tall, slim, looking better
> in a swimming costume than I do and running
> gleefully all over creation with my toddler son – I
> think of a bowed little woman with a grey perm,
> slippers and a faint smell of ammonia hanging
> apologetically in the air. (Lucy Mangan)[11]

The confusion and ambiguity over age expressed in this
extract are not unusual. Increasing healthy life expectancy
and changing expectations mean that many of the stereotypes
associated with old age are no longer applicable to most of
us over retirement age.

The people we interviewed did not identify themselves as
old. For example, Amelia (64) said: "I never think of myself
as an older person. When I go to see a band that was popular
when I was young I look around and think my God, they
are so old, but I'm like that too." And Mita, who is a similar
age, said: "I belong to U3A [the University of the Third
Age] and the first time I went to one of their meetings, I saw
a room full of 250 old people, I thought 'what am I doing
here?' but some of them were younger than me." For many
older people their ageing appearance is like a mask held
in front of them, while their younger self-image remains
intact behind it. The image of ageing as a mask describes
the discrepancy between how these individuals feel inside
and their outward appearance.[12] This may not be true for
everyone, since attitude and health play important parts in
the discontinuity older people experience between their
chronological age and their subjective or psychological age.
Jack, now in his early 70s, commented:

"I don't think about people as older if they are saying interesting things and are part of modern life and progress. I think that only stops happening when you are very old and frail. Now generally speaking that would be in your 80s. I would say that middle age goes on until 80 as long as you are doing all the things that you want to do. I know I'll feel it when I can't play golf and read etc. If you can do all the things you want you don't feel old."

It seems that the understanding and the boundaries of old age have shifted, at least for those people whose chronological age is 'old', although perhaps not for those who are younger Our interviewees were swift to point out that the old are not just one group, although as Lucy Mangan comments above, there is a tendency for the stereotype to be applied to anyone whose age is over a certain benchmark.

So where does this take us?

The media, and the visual media in particular, offer us a limited view of what it means to be older, tending to focus on limited stereotypes, with no recognition of diversity. The obsession with the youthful image can mean that older people are written out and side-lined, or cast as either dependent and frail, white-haired oldsters or the rare glamorous exception. The stress in the media is on looks alone. Catherine Westwood commented:

"It's interesting that I have been talking about ageing as aesthetic as opposed to being wise and having life experience. We should think and communicate that, but it seems to me that women are intrinsically linked to their looks."

The stress on outward appearance is perhaps inevitable in the visual media, but is there any way in which the emphasis on youthful beauty can be addressed? Within the market of 40+ women there is an increasing recognition that older women look attractive in their own right and that some of their life experience is relevant to this. Diane Kenwood, editor of *Woman's Weekly*, which appeals to a mass market of older women, thought that things were changing:

> "It is partly the things the readers say to us, but also, just take for example The Great British Bake Off final, it featured three celebrities, Dame Edna Everage and Joanna Lumley and Lulu, three more gloriously confident older 'women' you could not hope to find. It was a wonderful example of older people. The single most respected broadcaster is David Attenborough, and look how old he is? Age does not matter if people are passionate and wonderful about what they do. A lot of my judgement is instinct. In espousing the cause of older people I have sometimes felt I was pushing water uphill, but not so much now."

Perhaps there is the beginning of a change, meaning that older people are slightly more likely to be valued and respected at least in certain niche areas of the media. Diane Kenwood perceived this gradual change: "Even three years ago I would not have been so hopeful about how age is perceived, but now I see a change happening."

There is also an increased demand from older people to see themselves represented in the visual media. Sonia from Iceland, in her early 60s, commented:

> "It was late last year as I was about to begin watching a movie on TV that I realised that I had had more than I could take of teenage and young people's love stories and felt too old and weary to

try and relate to them any longer. The sad truth is
that there are very few programmes on Icelandic
TV which focus on elderly/old people."

Perhaps in response to the growth of an older audience and
their understandable wish to see more people like themselves
depicted, there have been more films and television
programmes in recent years with older people in central roles.
There have been stories in the media of sexual attraction
among older people, even those who are in care homes; for
example, the 2006 film *Away from Her* starred Julie Christie
as a woman with dementia who falls in love with a fellow
resident, and the TV success *Last Tango in Halifax* showed
an older couple happily in love, although there remains
something of a taboo on showing actual physical contact.

The success of the programme *Last Tango in Halifax*, and
of films like *Quartet* or the *Best Exotic Marigold Hotel* series,
indicates that film and programme makers are becoming
more aware of the important over-50s market and increased
coverage of older generations may begin to impact positively
on the wider population. A more focused but exciting
example of reimagining the image of older people, discussed
further in the next chapter, is the New Dynamics of Ageing
project 'Look at Me!' where older women were encouraged
to create their own images of ageing in art workshops.[13]

There are now even a few examples of older gay people in
films and books. Bernadette (66), commenting on the film
Grandma, was delighted that the main character "is a feisty
ex-academic, lesbian poet, out of work, broke, funny, kind,
and wise". She commented that it was a "new take on the
grandma role". Ignoring even more stereotypes, the novel
Mr Loverman is the story of an elderly, black gay man who
lives as a family man in East London but questions the need
to remain in the closet and 'comes out' to his son.[14]

There have also been public campaigns to address negative images of older people, for example, a billboard campaign in Melbourne, Australia to 'Look past the wrinkles' and a similar initiative in Madrid to promote positive attitudes towards the elderly.[15] Perhaps there is a slow and gradual recognition that the old constitute a valid part of society, with current generations of older people less likely to consign themselves to the margins and who want entertainment that features a more realistic representation of themselves.

What needs to change?

As we saw in the previous chapter, the role of older people in the workplace is changing, but there is strong evidence of entrenched ageism when it comes to working in the media, particularly for older women. There is beginning to be recognition that this is happening, but the combination of ageism and sexism is a difficult one to overcome.

We need a new look at old age.

Increased life expectancy, the increase in the proportion of older people in our society and the diversity of their situations mean that old-fashioned media stereotypes denigrating older people, seeing them only as dependent and consigning them to the side-lines are less applicable than they ever were. Current generations of older people want to see themselves represented more realistically in the media. Although the media focus mainly on the young, things are beginning to change. Although featuring some exceptional older women as 'the face' of a cosmetic brand may be about accessing a growing and lucrative market of older women, the use of older models will have a positive impact on all our perceptions of the old.

There is an iterative relationship between the individual and the media. Our view of ourselves as individuals is mediated through our culture, and media images of the old as predominantly dowdy, needy and frail can impact negatively on the individual's self-image as they reach older age A gradual cultural change fuelled by the occasional glamorous image of an older person, but backed up by older people's having different expectations, longer healthy life expectancy and greater economic clout, is beginning to influence the media presentation of the old, which then in turn contributes to a better self-image for older people. Could this be a widening virtuous circle?

EIGHT

Cover up

How early does the cover-up start? The 'horrifying' headline 'Pageant Mom Gives Botox to 8-Year-Old' reveals the story of a mother administering Botox to hide her daughter's wrinkles. On YouTube, daughter Britney said: 'It hurts sometimes and I cry ... when it is done I look beautiful.'[1] We describe this story as 'horrifying' because we see it as an extreme form of cultural oppression and Britney's forced treatment as barbaric. Our culture is oppressive in its construction of beauty, especially in how women should look. The ideal is to stay looking young and perfect.

In this chapter we uncover different reactions to the view that looking old is not desirable, and examine the extent to which people try to hide signs of age. We look at contrasting views – why some spend their lives attempting to avoid looking old, while some challenge what they see as cultural oppression and others see cosmetics and treatments as empowering. We draw on a range of respondents both within and outside our survey, including younger people, to examine:

- images and oppression – how beauty ideals dominate many women's lives in their belief that ageing is like a disease that can be cured;
- images and exploitation – the ways the cosmetic industry, magazines and the media exploit women's and men's fears by creating and advertising expensive products that claim to defy signs of ageing, using celebrities to endorse spurious claims; and
- images and liberation – we report on community and art projects that celebrate older people's bodies and a campaign challenging the cosmetic industry.

Images and oppression: why cover up?

Britney's story illustrates that youth in our culture is associated with physical perfection – flawless skin, colourful hair, slim bodies and sexiness. In stark contrast, older bodies, particularly women's, are associated with dry, wrinkled skin and grey hair. Older people are asexual.

Ageing bodies are despised in our society as the discussion of media exclusion in the previous chapter illustrates. Cartoons mock sagging bodies. Insults abound and greeting cards showing women's dangling breasts are found to be hilarious.

In our culture many people consider that covering ugly signs of ageing through surgical and non-surgical interventions and cosmetics is both normal and essential. Our own investigations reveal a range of perceptions. A continuum emerges from the 'cosmetic compulsives' to the 'rouge renouncers'. Midway along are the preservers, the colourists and the conservers. The strategies that people adopt may start in their younger years as a response to negative images of ageing.

The continuum includes:

- compulsives who use everything
- preservers who stop short of surgery
- colourists who cover grey hair and apply make-up
- conservers who use moisturisers
- renouncers who use nothing.

The compulsives seek a cure. They crave perfection, buy expensive products that promise eternal youth, use surgical and non-surgical interventions in the hope of 'defying' age. They spend a fortune seeking the perfect combination of treatments.

Hannah, just in her 30s, is a compulsive. On a television programme she catalogued her treatments, starting with a nose job at 17, Botox at 18.[2] She continues to have treatments in order 'to feel confident', despite the health risks. Hannah seeks perfection and youthfulness.

The 'preservers' believe they will be helped to stay young-looking, especially by Botox. It was reported on the same television programme that featured Hannah that groups of young women hold 'Botox parties' where they inject each other in the pursuit of eternal youth. Botox has become normalised. Two factors encourage this trend: the culture of celebrity and treatment being more accessible. In the UK in 2015 a staggering £3.6 billion was spent on treatments. Selling Botox online is unregulated and its use can have serious side-effects. Bizarrely, women and men are risking their health to avoid looking their age. 'Preservers' use creams and potions to ensure youthful skin. Martha (50) explained to us:

> "I spend at least an hour a day using different products. I haven't found anything that is really good and I'm disappointed. Each product promises youthful skin but I see no real improvement."

Colourists have a different outlook. They talk of fun. Marj (69) said to us in a somewhat bashful way:

> "I used to be called a lipstick lesbian. I still paint my nails. I like experimenting. Now nearly 70, I still have my hair highlighted and use bronzing cream to give my face colour."

Mable (103), who was the oldest person we spoke to, talked about how she enhances her looks:

> "I was brought up to believe I needed to make the best of myself. My mother told me I would never get a husband if I didn't take care. Even at my ripe old age I still use make-up otherwise I wouldn't feel dressed. I wear different make-up when I go dancing. I love my purple eye shadow as it brings out the blue of my eyes and I wear plenty of rouge. I am shocked that other women let themselves go."

Flora (58) told us that many women like her "just enjoy the pleasures of being a woman, being feminine, wanting to wear nice clothes and make-up to feel and look good":

> "My grey hair doesn't bother me, but I enjoy make-up and I am careful about my weight from a health point of view. Some people see that as frivolous – this can be seen as giving in to the dominant culture. My motives are misinterpreted."

Flora acts without a sense of obligation to wear make-up but is aware that others think she is influenced by the dominant view of what a woman should look like. But for her it is a choice. She said, half-jokingly: "I have been thinking about what I'd like to see in your book – daft things like a page on keeping skin nice."

Grey is a common metaphor for ageing. Some, like Bernadette (66), started colouring their hair in their teens and are not going to stop. Reporting to us that "Grey hair just doesn't suit me", Bernadette wants to keep the same identity, maintaining continuity with "an earlier self", as other researchers have found.[3] Veronica (58) wants to escape the image of old: "I colour my hair because I don't like looking in the mirror and seeing an old dull person," she said to us. Hair colouring seems more acceptable than other interventions, as Kate (65) explained: "I certainly don't approve of surgery as I see it as an extreme form of not accepting oneself. However, I do dye my hair, saying to myself it's for fun. But I'm probably trying to preserve my youth."

Going grey is a significant threshold and many are happy to accept it. Ruth (64) said:

> "I still want to have edge and style – I try to be different, while also being myself, with a funky haircut. I don't want to become that elderly woman who's gone to the other extreme, and is so 'out there' that she loses all dignity."

Grey hair on men is often considered distinguished, conferring authority and dignity. Colouring their hair is unnecessary.

The 'conservers' were the most prominent group in our survey, acknowledging that it is impossible to stop the ageing process but wanting to avoid dry, uncomfortable skin. Maureen (80) said this was what she most disliked about getting older. Essential moisturisers are the beauty products most frequently used by the over-60s, a survey reported.[4]

Some women justified using carefully selected products to boost their sense of well-being, fully realising that the promises of the cosmetic industry are not genuine. Jo (58) said in her interview with us: "I'm not taken in by the ads that say creams can stop the ageing process – it's nonsense. But I buy moisturisers to make my skin feel nice."

The 'rouge renouncers' are indifferent. Veronica (58) told us that

> "Apart from soap and shampoo the amount I spend on beauty products is minimal. I get a jar of cream every few years to stop my lips chapping. I haven't time for any of that rubbish. I find it inexplicable that there is so much emphasis on hiding ageing."

Veronica represents the view of those who recognise dominant cultural oppression and refuse to be manipulated by advertising and broader media messages.

However, other researchers have highlighted a difficulty for some women in owning their 'agedness' and retaining confidence as they age.[5] In her interview with us Cindy (50) expressed a similar view:

> "I am surprised by my thickening midriff [laughs]. I am naturally slim and doing my best to stay like that but I'm pre-menopausal and it creeps up. My body is starting to change and I don't want it to."

Miriam (69) also revealed to us similar disquiet: "I have lost weight and have been horrified by the change in the quality of my skin which suddenly looks like that of a genuinely old woman. I can't bear to look in the mirror naked." Here are echoes of the struggles with the betrayals of the body, the skin becoming an alien structure.[6] This deterioration has led to some authors to refer to a dehumanising function, leading to the consideration of older people as a separate species.[7]

Intellectually, many consider ageing a natural process, but these examples demonstrate that people's emotions can have a profoundly negative effect. Flora (58) explained: "When I look at older people it can be deeply depressing to see what's ahead. I need to take care of myself. It's my investment in the future to stay healthy as long as possible. I go swimming, exercise and stay slim." For many women youthfulness, beauty and fitness are inextricably linked.

Conflicting attitudes towards different stances

During the interviews we noted subtle or highly judgemental attitudes towards others' views on covering the signs of ageing. Mable said, "I am shocked that other women let themselves go." The pressure to use cosmetics is strong and our research reveals that even the most intelligent women can't resist the inducement to stay looking young. Magazine editor Catherine Westwood pointed out to us that:

> "Women are intrinsically linked to their looks. It's a brave woman who says I am not going to dye my hair, not going to make an effort. We are brought up to have a sense of duty about looking good."

Other research reveals that women who refuse to use 'anti-ageing' products are at risk of being labelled 'deviant' or 'apathetic'.[8] This research revealed that women's failure to engage in such practices may be seen as 'a sign of disturbed gender identity and low self-esteem', rather than showing resistance to oppressive norms of behaviour.

However, some feminist researchers, for example, assert that beauty work can be liberating for women of all ages, arguing that it provides opportunities for self-expression and the reclamation of power.[9] For example, research on make-up practices suggests that 'in creating effects through makeup, and more generally in learning how to wear makeup, women emerge as active creators and elaborators of the self'.[10]

Supporting this stance, further research claims that, rather than being conned by misogynist appearance norms, women are seen as 'canny cultural negotiators who choose to use beauty work to their own advantage'.[11] Opinions are divided. While some of us are shocked by this perspective, others are convinced that it is the right thing to do.

The issue we have with this standpoint is that it denies any hope of shifting cultural attitudes in seeing beauty in age. A passionate plea is made by Bridget Christie:

> If we don't start valuing ourselves as more than just a commodity, and stop basing all our happiness and success on how we look, all the progress we've made will be a complete waste of time. What's the point of holding up a mirror to female oppression if we can't even look in it ourselves.[12]

The social objectification of women leads to self-defeating attempts to stay looking young. Societal pressure is strong, particularly for women – a point that Pedro (55) raised when talking with us:

> "Why do people persist in kidding themselves? What's wrong with ageing, looking old, or just looking your age? I see beauty in age. I believe more women than men succumb to cosmetic or surgical intervention, so often, in my view, with disastrous, if not laughable consequences. Is it peer pressure?"

The perspective of 'seeing beauty in age' is gaining ground. Tina (55) agrees and made it clear to us how her views and feelings have changed as she gets older:

> "I promised myself a facelift at 50, but after I gave up a high-pressured job I discovered I didn't want one. I don't look so tired. Now I'm frustrated by anti-wrinkle cream ads, as if having wrinkles is a bad thing. I get angry. When I think back to wanting a facelift I'm ashamed for not realising I'd been sucked into believing a commercially driven construct about how women should look."

This is exactly what some feminist researchers argue:

> dominant images of the ideal female body serve to oppress women suggesting they are victims of false consciousness;

and

> women judge their own appearances against feminine beauty ideals. As they age they are found sorely lacking.[13]

Gail (45) felt that the issue could be viewed in two ways. She said to us:

> "If someone wants to use cosmetics as a way to look after themselves and feel good then I am all for it. If they are using them because they don't feel good enough or presentable without them then it's coming from a place of deficit. That's sad."

Let's not forget the men

There is a double standard. It is widely believed that men stay more attractive than women as they age. Catherine Westwood said to us that:

> "Men are faced with different pressures. It seems to be that women and men have a completely different set of rules. It is OK to be George Clooney and to be grey and ageing but not for women. They [women] tend to need bits and pieces doing to hold back the years."

But advertising has recently focused on the male body, creating new myths of masculine beauty. For example, a survey revealed a generation of men befuddled with feelings of inadequacy, emasculated by images of David Beckham and Daniel Craig 'in the buff'.[14]

Our male interviewees did not express concern about their looks but Don (72) mentioned different pressures. He was concerned about the loss of libido that had taken him by surprise: "This is an undiscussed issue. Our need for intimacy continues while our physical means of expressing it are taken away."

Chris Gilleard confirms that 'men traditionally have expressed less concern, in public, over their bodily appearance, focussing instead upon issues of potency and performance'.[15] Internet searches reveal many sites selling 'cheap Viagra'. Men are also putting their health at risk by buying unregulated products.

In our analysis of fashion magazines we note that men are advised to keep their bellies flat, keep fit, stay moisturised, try dental whitening and shave off scraggly beards. Baldness appears a big issue, with jokes about wigs ('scalp rugs'), hairpieces and bizarre comb-overs ridiculing men's attempts to disguise their hair loss, although in our interviews no one mentioned this.

Men spend less than women on looking good, but their spending is increasing. Mintel, the market research company, reported that the UK's beauty and personal care market was worth £16.6 billion in 2014, and forecast that consumers would spend an average of £342 in 2015 on beauty and skin care alone. Men's skin-care products are rising in popularity, estimated at £96 million in the same period.[16]

There is strong peer and societal pressure to stay looking young and fit, for both sexes, and a huge amount of money is made from cosmetics. This is a highly lucrative business.

Images and exploitation: the business of the cosmetic industry

The cosmetic industry is thriving (estimated to reach over £180 billion globally by 2015), as many believe that interventions will help them to stay looking young. Images of beauty are used to undermine both women and men and make them feel vulnerable. The industry can then sell gullible people the products that it tells them they need in order to restore their feelings of value.[17] It exploits insecurities by encouraging men and women to keep monitoring themselves for signs of imperfection. Some argue that this process results in, and reinforces, social subordination in an ageist and sexist society.[18] Media images of slim and ageless women further perpetuate a beauty ideal that marginalises older women while providing them with tools to mask the signs of ageing.[19]

Molly Andrews says that the concept of agelessness erases our experience, strips us of our history and leaves nothing but mimicry of our youth.[20] She says that the challenges of ageing are many and real and that to deny them in an attempt to counter ageing is folly.

The industry operates in different ways. It uses celebrities to endorse its brands, and invents pseudo-scientific language to describe its products. It attaches ludicrous claims to products, such as 'time delay', 'anti-ageing' and 'age-defying'. It creates vloggers who demonstrate the use of make-up to cover signs of ageing, and they become celebrities themselves – famous for their skills in creating agelessness. The industry occasionally draws on 'real people' to present and promote more realistic and acceptable images. These are women who have tried and failed to cover signs of ageing but have now discovered a new miracle cure. The industry is highly effective in its work, as the amount spent on products continues to rise.

Below, we examine two aspects: one, the direct commercial activity of the industry in its advertising; and two, indirect support of the industry in magazines and popular media coverage, the latter having a wider influence on our culture.

Advertising

The cosmetic industry, in its advertising, is about persuading people that it is really not desirable to look over 40. It exploits people's fears of losing their youthful looks by advertising expensive products that claim to 'defy' signs of ageing.

Advertisements exploit the idea that the whole appearance of a person is an important statement. It is what people are judged on – whether they are poor, rich, fat, thin, attractive or ugly. It matters how we look and the possession of visible signs of poor health, cognitive and physical loss and advanced age are increasingly socially detrimental.[21]

Older people are used in advertisements to demonstrate the awfulness of ageing 'naturally' and how that decline can be eradicated, or at least arrested, by the use of cosmetic products. The most beautiful and highly successful actors and celebrities are showcased in advertisements. But, rather than appealing just to younger women, the industry differentiates the market in order to boost sales.

Older women are now employed to attract the over-60s, recently seen as a lucrative market worth cultivating. The actress Charlotte Rampling, 69, has become the face of NARS, and Helen Mirren, 70, of L'Oréal Paris. We admire Mirren's attitude in insisting that her images are not retouched to cover wrinkles. She said, 'The great thing that happens as you age is that you don't really give a flying fuck.'[22]

L'Oréal's own research shows that half of women over 50 feel overlooked, even though they hold more of the country's wealth and spend more on products than younger women do.[23] But Catherine Westwood talked to us of its being tokenism: "It is the advertiser thinking 'we can get publicity because we are using an older person'."

But it is all a confidence trick, whether the images are of younger or older women. The advertisements fail to tell the public that most images are air-brushed to perfection.

Magazines

The fashion, beauty and gossip magazines are packed with stories about who looks good. They follow the lives of the stars and comment on face-lifts that have been done and those who have had Botox.

Another disturbing characteristic in some media is the unconcealed pleasure derived when people commit cosmetic blunders or fall from perfection – Schadenfreude or gloating – celebrating others' misfortunes. They are triumphant and gain malicious satisfaction from their reporting. This is often about weight – television stars who had lost six stones and then regained it. The 'before' and 'after' photos the magazines publish are humiliating. They also show, in graphic detail, the after-effects of surgery that has gone wrong. Catherine Westwood explained to us why these stories are popular:

"The press has a line in 'how awful/old she looks' when they show pictures of famous women looking a bit tired. We all have bad days. But readers tend to like that kind of article because celebs look worse than us."

An example of such a story appeared on the front page of one newspaper.[24] The headline read: 'Oh Kate, are you really showing grey roots at 33?' There was a huge photo with the offending grey hair brightly circled just in case a reader might miss the horror. On page 7 the story continued: 'If you have ever felt envious of The Duchess of Cambridge's glossy chestnut mane this picture might provide some comfort. For it shows that even beautiful young royals are not immune to the ageing process.' Kate's neglecting to colour her hair was put down to the fact that she was pregnant and avoiding the use of chemicals. There had to be a compelling reason for this, it seems. Catherine Westwood said:

"Women are damned either way. Newspapers celebrate young, nubile women and to a lesser degree older women who have managed to preserve their looks – but if they have too much surgery they are derided for trying to maintain their youth."

But there are some surprising views on the extent to which women would like to be improved. Catherine Westwood continued:

"There was an interesting piece I saw in *Woman* magazine. They had pictures of women as they are now and had scanned in pictures showing how they would look with fewer wrinkles and then with even fewer, sort of de-aged. When asked which they preferred most chose the one *immediately before* their actual age. It is an insight into how women want to see themselves – just a *little* bit better."

Images and liberation: celebrating older people's bodies

On the nights of 4 and 5 November 2014 huge images of older women appeared on Sheffield city's most famous buildings:

> Kathleen and Eleanor, in big hair and sunglasses, covered the City Hall. Jill's wrinkles, teeth and grey hair were beamed onto the side of the Town Hall. Shirley, taking off her wig, featured on the side of the Library in Tudor Square.

The New Dynamics of Ageing 'Look at Me!' project circulated these images.[25] Lorna Warren, who led the project at the University of Sheffield, explained in the project's report that: 'Women aged 50 and over make up over a quarter (27.4%) of Sheffield's population, yet we rarely see any representations of them or their lives.' The women involved in the project, aged between 41 and 93, examined media portrayals and then produced their own images to capture their experiences of ageing.

- Kathleen and Eleanor poked fun at the 'before-and-after' format of make-overs.
- Jill portrayed the ambiguity of ageing: 'Some days I feel OK and some days I see myself and I think who is that?'
- Shirley set out to capture the pleasure of dressing up – 'I like a bit of glam' – but, after taking off her costume, realised she was happy as she was.

- Hermi has her legs up on her motorised scooter: 'The silver lining in old age is that you can do what you like.'

Commenting on the project, in her role of photographer, Rosy Martin wrote:

> It was turning 50 that made me want to explore how the dominant representations of older women showed only stereotypes of decline and redundancy. I wanted to challenge this, and find ways of representing my ageing self through my photographic practice in a subversive, playful and resistant way.[26]

For all those who participated in the 'Look at Me!' project, it was a liberating and transformative experience, leaving them with an enhanced self-image and having benefited from working collaboratively. One participant commented: 'I'd like people to come away with the impression of the energy that was there – the creativity, vitality, all-round feistiness of women of our age ... I'd like to give people a sense of what society is missing really by making us invisible.'[27]

As a phototherapist, Rosy Martin explores the relationships between photography, memory, identities and unconscious processes. Her work makes explicit the multiplicity of identities that an individual inhabits, using the 'self' as a text to be deconstructed, reviewed, challenged and reconsidered. The importance of her work is that it breaks through the stereotype of beauty, including seeing beauty in ageing bodies – an important and recurring theme.

The ground-breaking work of Jo Spence in representing realistic images of people is also to be celebrated. Her early photographs challenged the idealised imagery of advertising. Women's bodies in particular were her interest – sick as well as healthy. Her later works, especially self-portraits, were about breast cancer. Through her phototherapy she expressed her powerlessness as a patient. By documenting her experiences she was an active agent rather than a passive object. The value of this approach is that it forces people to look at disfigurement and challenge ideas about youth, beauty and perfection.

A shift in our thinking is needed. Anne Karpf suggests that 'Each time we see an older person we need to imagine them as our future self and rather than recoil from their wrinkles or infirmities applaud their resilience.'[28] We have noticed, over the last five years while researching for this book, that attitudes are changing.

- Initiatives such as the Sheffield 'Look at Me!' project aim to transform the way society views older women in their refusal to pathologise age.
- There is enlightenment expressed by the magazine editor we quote, who talks of a duty of care and responsibility to readers. Her focus is on ageing naturally rather than anti-ageing.
- Many actresses are speaking out against the use of Botox, claiming that they are determined to age naturally, including Jane Seymour, 63, Jacqueline Bisset, 69[29] and Emma Thompson, 54.[30]

We also notice that academic thinking and dialogue continues. For example, in April 2016, at the Royal Academy in London, feminist academic Lynne Segal and art historian Aileen Ribeiro examined the representation of ageing alongside attitudes towards age and beauty.

Cleaning up its act?

There is good news in the way pressure is being put on the cosmetic industry to change. We watched the Dove YouTube sequence with amazement. It shows how the liquify tool in Photoshop, carrying out body-shape editing, transforms a perfectly lovely model into an air-brushed beauty with huge, uplifted eyes and skinny contours. The caption 'No wonder our perception of beauty is distorted' signifies this grotesque misrepresentation.

Unilever launched the Dove 'Campaign for Real Beauty' in 2004. It includes advertisements, videos, workshops, a book and a play. The aim is to celebrate the natural physical variation embodied by all women and to inspire them to have the confidence to be comfortable with their looks.

Like all other manufacturers, Unilever's aim is to make money, but it provides a significant shift in redefining the standards of advertising and challenges the unrealistic ideals about the way women should look. The main message for women is to be content with their looks and not worry about conforming to an idealised image. Some people believe that Dove's images are still not representative enough – still too sexy and too slim. From the consumer's perspective the Dove campaign was 'phenomenally successful'. A director of consumer research told us: "It is always mentioned by consumers, especially the YouTube video."

What needs to change?

Through a process of unlearning we can come to see beauty in age. Some of the most brilliant artists throughout history have portrayed older people respectfully and beautifully. We can all learn from this.

Magazines, newspapers and other media need to respect older people and recognise a duty of care and responsibility to their readers.

The spurious claims made by advertisers must be challenged.

There needs to be a focus on ageing naturally, rather than anti-ageing, and on ridding society of the nonsensical view that ageing is like a disease that can be cured.

We need to challenge the dominant representations of older people, showing only stereotypes of decline and redundancy. We need to follow the example set by the feisty, age-celebrating women in Sheffield who, in making themselves visible, uncover multifaceted, powerful and distinctive identities.

NINE

Everybody's gotta
be somewhere!

'Everybody's gotta be somewhere' was a truth observed by Spike Milligan on *The Goon Show*. But there has been a housing shortage in the UK for decades. All eyes are usually on young people struggling to get onto the ladder but, according to a DEMOS report, the next housing crisis is the chronic undersupply of appropriate housing for older people.[1] The shortage has implications for national policy and for local neighbourhoods. Decent housing makes a huge difference to individuals' and families' well-being and to good relationships.

Because the bricks and mortar of homes also represent the wealth or capital of those who own them, issues about housing are compounded with financial and investment dimensions. In the UK, discussion about homes and housing is a conversation about wealth and class.

As far as the growing older population is concerned, public discussion is largely focused on residential care for the frailest. The next chapter looks at the provision for these people. The specific needs of those who do not yet, and perhaps never will, require residential care are largely ignored. We need more accommodation, including for rent, suitable for single people and adaptable for independent living.

Two matters concern us in this chapter. First, home and community become increasingly important as people get older. Home is a place of belonging, comfort, safety, personal and family history. Policy focuses on providing housing, not on the larger concept of home or community. Second, the community within which the home is situated plays a major part in contributing to a person's well-being.

In this chapter we consider the issues for older people who wish to remain independent and introduce some innovative housing arrangements that can help to meet the needs of this age group. Our vision for the future is of a proliferation of age-integrated housing, planned and developed by local communities.

What is changing?

The ageing revolution is changing the issues and presenting new housing challenges. More people are living longer and want to find ways to remain independent for longer.

Moving into institutional care is happening later in life, if at all. Only 3.7% of people over 65 live in residential accommodation. Because dependence happens later, the need increases for more appropriate housing as people remain 'in place' for longer.

We need more housing, and more for single people. We need to provide the adaptations and community support required for longer to ensure well-being among older residents.

Independence is what many older people say they want

Fears of institutional care in old age have deep historical roots. The separation of married couples, punitive conditions and public shame contributed to the fear. Workhouses were abolished in 1929 but the fear of the workhouse persisted until after the Second World War for those unable to care for themselves.[2]

Fears about present-day institutional care may make people reluctant to make the move. More significant is the desire for independence: making one's own decisions, having privacy and control. The people we interviewed all wanted to avoid dependence on others, in particular on their families.

Atul Gawande, in his book *Being Mortal*, reminds us about the strength of this desire to remain at home, through the story of his wife's grandmother in America.[3] Alice Hobson was very reluctant to leave her home after a long and independent life, 'the one place where she felt she belonged and remained in charge of her life'. Despite excellent facilities in the care home, she said 'It just isn't home'. She was under surveillance, albeit benign surveillance: the staff monitored her health and her diet and supervised her medication. Atul Gawande uses the telling image of a foreign country to highlight Alice's situation:

> For Alice, it must have felt as if she had crossed into an alien land that she would never be allowed to leave. The border guards were friendly and cheerful enough. They promised her a nice place to live where she'd be well taken care of. But she didn't really want anyone to take care of her; she just wanted to live a life of her own. And those cheerful border guards had taken her keys and her passport. With her home went her control.

Home is a place of comfort and belonging, but the very people who might initially make it possible to age in your own home, your family, may eventually not be able to bear the burden. A care nurse (Alice) provided us with some extracts from her diaries. She wrote about an old woman she cared for in a local hospital. One day Vera was visited by her daughters and later became very distressed.

> Now that her daughters had left, Vera was angry. Gone was the sweet, smiley docile old lady from before. She was off with her Zimmer frame, raging round the corridors, expressing her defiance in every way she could: refusing her medicine, refusing to go to the toilet, trying to get through doors that she shouldn't go through. And everyone she met was a daughter to whom she expressed her intense displeasure.
>
> "How could you do this to me? – that's what I don't understand. All I want is to have a quiet corner at home, just to be at home where I belong. What have I done to deserve this? How could you be so selfish? I'm perfectly capable of looking after myself. I don't want to be here: I hate this place ..."
> Over the years I have met hundreds of Veras, all longing to go home.

Vera's anger and defiance came from being cared for outside her home. One of our interviewees had an interesting idea about financial benefits for families involved with elder care. Dayo (58), brought up in Nigeria, is a believer in family responsibilities and she suggested that "government should give financial support to families caring for older people".

> "The thinking about care for older people needs viewing from a different perspective and I

think the responsibility should be that of family members. Just as government provides help to parents in terms of child support and benefits, government should give financial support to families caring for older people. That way some of the issues of abuse old people suffer at care homes will no longer arise or be drastically reduced. People may say they don't want to finish raising their children only to start nursing their parents but that is shirking of responsibilities and though it might take some convincing they will be glad they did. Not only will they see the benefits in the well-being of their elderly parents but they'll appreciate it more when it's their turn and they enjoy being looked after by their own children."

This is an interesting alternative approach, but we should not assume that elder abuse does not occur in families. Nor should we assume that all older people would be happy to be cared for by their family, and not everyone has children.

Some challenges to ageing independently

Despite the strong desire to age independently, it is not without difficulties for the state, the community, the families and for the individuals themselves.

Costs of support

Local communities have an important role to play in helping older people to remain independent for longer, interviewees told us. Hannah (54), a retired district nurse, referred to the expense for individuals and the state of more care of older people in their own homes.

Pauline (74), a retired GP, also recognised the cost of providing care as well as training and support for care workers:

> "[We need an] increase in supported and residential care and in support to help people at home. Proper 'care packages' should not only be in place but the staff funding for this should be there at the same time. This would prevent many readmissions to homes and hospitals. Carers should be properly trained but also told to use their common sense – no jobsworths."

We look at care more fully in the next chapter.

Supporting people to age with independence will require a combination of commercial activity and much volunteer work. It is not a cheap alternative to residential care. Rather, it is an argument for listening to the expressed desires of older people and finding ways to meet them.

Family responsibilities

Duty and capacity may be in tension for families trying to support an older person. Many family members experience ambivalence about what is best for an elderly relative, as it is demanding and likely to become more difficult over time. Other family needs compete: maintaining jobs, other family relationships, the financial demands of children and the necessity of taking holidays. Loving relationships can be tested severely by the demands of care. Catherine (63) reminded us that the older person may also experience ambivalence, knowing that they need more support and not wanting to need it.

People like to imagine that families take care of their older relatives as a matter of course in other cultures and that this used to be the case in the UK. While many, many people willingly care for older relatives, we cannot build a future on the expectation that families will undertake this care. The limits of families' capacities mean that arguments for community support for older people who live at home are strong. Many, many people provide both informal and formal support for their neighbours. Already there are an unknowable quantity of neighbours who do shopping, share social moments, provide transport, fix things, offer advice and so forth. There are volunteer organisations that provide considerable support, often in collaboration with the local health provider, especially befriending and transport to hospitals. Issues of who does the caring and what that means for our ageing society are examined in the next chapter.

Loneliness

The isolated older person is often invisible, perhaps lacking the mobility or the confidence to emerge from their home. Loneliness may be the biggest challenge to the well-being of the old. A third of people over 65 live in one-person households.[4] The divorce rate is increasing (8.7% in 2011) among people who are 65+ years old. Living alone is often not a matter of choice, especially for women, who live longer and are less likely to find a new partner in old age.[5] The risk of isolation is therefore greater for them and it is possible that it accounts for the fall in ratings of personal well-being by people over 75.[6] Of course, a person can also be lonely living with other people.

Maureen (80) quoted her aunt, who had a positive attitude to loneliness:

> "Loneliness is a terrible thing, but my aunt always
> said, you never need to be lonely while you have

a roof over your head. You can always invite
people in."

It isn't always easy to invite people in, especially if there are
difficulties with mobility. Befriending volunteers have an
important role here. Sometimes befriending is organised, or
happens through formal social contacts, such as through the
U3A, which promotes sharing of interests in people's homes.

Age segregation

One option on offer is the retirement communities where
people live in their own houses or flats restricted to a certain
age group. These are often gated, controlled entry perhaps
increasing feelings of security. It is more cost-effective to
group together people of the same age, for medical and social
services for example. But communities do not necessarily
thrive on similarities in age, which may range over 20 years –
and why would they? Shared interests and concerns are more
likely to create good social bonds. For some, the segregation
by age is an anathema. We have reported elsewhere that
Ruth, who is in her mid-60s, wants to live in the community
as long as possible and among a mix of ages.

Where there is additional care, retirement villages appear
to enhance the quality of life for the residents. They report
less isolation and loneliness, good feelings of independence,
and enjoy the on-site care and company.[7]

There is a need to build more suitable homes: only 533,000
retirement homes have been built and about 3.5 million
people, or 25% of people over 60, are interested in buying
such properties.[8]

Physical adaptations required

Some older people with mobility problems may want to live on one floor or install a stair lift. They may need adaptations for washing, using the toilet, cooking and so forth. These can be expensive, and are often not at all attractive or aesthetically pleasing. Better design for mobility aids, please! The Elderly Accommodation Council provides advice on adaptations and places for the elderly to live.[9]

Security and help on site

There is also a demand for accommodation that provides a range of on-call assistance and security. Devices that call for help are one version of this. Sheltered accommodation, with an on-site warden, is a more comprehensive version. For many this is a half-way stage between being independent and going into some kind of residential care. Although separate, it can be connected to the community and provide some social contacts for the residents.

What other people say older people should do

Those who blame the boomer generation for everything have not hesitated to find them culpable of creating and perpetuating the housing shortage. It is widely assumed that the 60+ age group bought their homes cheaply and have accrued considerable capital as a result, although many have outstanding mortgages.[10] Among people aged over 65 there is a wide range of housing tenure: 75% own their home and 24% are renting.[11] The situation for older people who rent is as bad as that for younger people.[12]

Exaggerating the wealth of over-65s leads the Intergenerational Institute to use emotive language, likening acquiring housing to stocking up on sugar at a time of shortage. Here are some quotations from *Hoarding of housing: The intergenerational crisis in the housing market*:[13]

- 'The current housing crisis is not principally about Britain having enough housing but about the way it is shared between older and younger generations.'
- 'There are now 25 million surplus bedrooms in under-occupied houses in England. "Hoarding of living space" (under-occupation) is increasing very rapidly.'
- 'The crisis in British housing has become politically destabilising as younger people increasingly consider that unfairness in this area is breaking the intergenerational pact.'

The report used unexamined assumptions that need challenging. Most people would see the housing crisis as a shortage of enough houses. There is also a shortage of smaller units suitable for older people, for the young and for the single; and accommodation in cities for young people, especially those in low-paid sectors of employment, has been recognised as a particular difficulty. The idea that a redistribution of housing between older and younger generations would solve these structural issues is simplistic and wrong.

The 25 million bedrooms may be surplus in the terms defined by the report, but many older people would not regard them in that way. They store possessions and provide short- and longer-term space for family and friends. They may use so-called spare rooms to provide space for their interests, to write or to paint. Couples may not want to share bedrooms. They may need the space to accommodate solutions to health issues, such as live-in carers and equipment.

Observer journalist Yvonne Roberts emphasised the importance of homes within the community in her debate with Shiv Malik on the report.[14]

> [This report's approach] ignores what it means to feel you belong, to have a sense of well-being, to be of use to your wider family. Or, to put it more simply, a home with a 'spare' bedroom is also a link to neighbours; an anchor to your community; a store of memories (a third of dementia sufferers live in their own home) and a means of support for yourself and your family.

We have already referred to the 3.5 million people over 60 who would consider moving into a smaller property if it existed. The same report indicated that about a third of over-60s would like to downsize – about 4.6 million people. The housing shortage makes it very difficult for them to move.[15]

Many parents have contributed to the accommodation needs of their offspring. An increasing number of young people remain living with their parents – up to 20% in the London area. We acknowledged in Chapter Three that the older generation have delayed giving an inheritance to their offspring by dying later. Gifts before death, however, have increased to such an extent that Piketty has called older age 'a golden age of gift-giving', mostly of property.[16]

Blaming the old masks the causes of and the complex solutions to the housing shortage. Since the Right to Buy was introduced by the Thatcher government, the public housing stock has been depleted. Councils were not allowed to use the receipts from sales to build new houses. And today, cash-strapped local authorities make alliances with house builders so that they both benefit from building homes for the rich – and a small amount is diverted to what are called 'affordable homes'. Shortages increase prices, so houses become investment vehicles: for small investors, rapidly rising prices mean that rent is profitable, and this is why Buy to Let is popular; for larger investors, including the foreign super-rich, houses are a store, a reserve currency.

Because houses are attached to land and suitable land is limited, increased demand has forced land prices to rise too. Builders and other landowners borrow against the land they own and developers wait to get a higher return on their investment, which does not encourage building of houses.

The housing shortage requires complex solutions. While financial and economic approaches are important, solutions must also take account of those important social aspects of the home that we have identified, especially for older people: people want places of independence, of belonging, of safety.

Age-friendly communities

Another factor that makes people reluctant to move is fear that a new environment may not suit them so well.[17] Suitable housing is important to quality of life, and so are the communities in which we live. We can break this idea down further and say that there are six factors in the environment that influence quality of life.[18] The order in which we present this research applies specifically to older people, but the factors are important to everyone in the community.

1. Having a role
2. Support networks
3. Income and wealth
4. Health
5. Having time
6. Independence

We find this a useful list to evaluate age-friendly neighbourhoods and the importance of the home within the community. When people move they can change the factors that influence their well-being. For example, networks take time to create, and without them people can feel lost and isolated. It is helpful to have mobility and some disposable income. Communities that promote all six factors would be good places for people to grow older.

People value their homes in part for the communities in which they are situated, and this increases with age. Statistics from the Office for National Statistics (ONS) indicate that 81% of people aged over 70 agreed that local friendships and associations meant a lot to them, as compared to 64% of those aged 50–54, who can make social contacts through their work.[19]

We see age-friendliness as an early stage of developing age-integrated communities. They have taken on board age-related issues and adopted features that qualify for the description of age friendly. Two things are apparent in such communities: first, that the benefits of taking account of older people include making communities better for people of all ages; and second, that small changes often have profound effects.

Attention is paid to these aspects:

- *Safety*: It is safe for people to come out of their homes and engage in community activities. Roads and pavements are maintained and well lit when it's dark, and good design and watchful neighbours reduce the risks and fears of crime. Health and social services are local and accessible.
- *Transport*: Public transport is free to older people, frequently available and coordinated, especially in rural areas. Bus passes and other preferential rates for older users promote the use of public transport and reduce isolation.
- *Community spaces, resources and facilities*: These are designed so that they are in easy reach of residential areas. Attention is paid to those small details that can make a big difference to everyone, such as traffic circulation, lighting, public toilets, benches.
- *Community activities*: These are organised to include older people, and some are led by older people. Some activities

may be dedicated, such as Memory Cafes to assist people whose memories are fading. The activities and spaces enable the older population to share their wisdom within the community.

- *Dementia awareness*: Some villages, towns and cities are taking steps towards becoming dementia friendly, such as Cirencester. The initiative, supported by the Alzheimer's Society since 2012, encourages people with dementia to contribute to and participate in meaningful activities; and those who care for them are encouraged to seek support. People who deal with the public, such as shop assistants, crossing attendants, community police and so forth, are trained in dementia awareness.

Wise communities include older people

We now take the idea of age-friendly neighbourhoods further, to consider the value of age-integrated and even wise communities. They go beyond age-friendliness, to be inclusive and to harness the wisdom of their members to benefit everyone, based on wise principles and wise processes. We do not adopt a simple or romantic idea that all old people are wise. In Chapter Thirteen, 'Wiser together', we explore fully how experience develops into wisdom. Here we explore the idea that some processes promote wise communities.

- *Inclusiveness*: Principles of democracy and inclusion are made explicit. Everyone is listened to, whatever their age. Different people's needs are identified and the community provides support.
- *Respectfulness*: Wise communities share the intent to do good for all through collaboration. People are treated with affection and everyone in the community is given authentic responsibilities for the care of others. Problematic situations

are defused with humour, and defensive posturing is met with warmth and patience.

- *Learning focus*: Participants are encouraged to add to community's knowledge base. Dialogue is the preferred method, generated and sustained in a collective and continuous way. Dialogue requires and reinforces trust and openness.
- *Curiosity and creativity*: Unconventional ideas and solutions – new realities – replace repetitive patterns.
- *Insightfulness*: Wisdom is recognised and made explicit and individuals are acknowledged for their wisdom and desire to do good (for example, people with skills and experience as reformers and visionary thinkers) and are called upon to help generate cohesion or well-being within the community.
- *Wisdom*: Wisdom becomes embedded in the ways that the community sees itself and operates. Leadership is shared and develops from the interaction between people, their common ethos, values and practices.

Here we provide a range of models and initiatives to illustrate what this looks like in practice, applied to local neighbourhoods. Chapter Thirteen provides examples of the principles in action in other ways.

In the **Home Share** scheme a young person is provided with accommodation in return for some domestic services and social contact with the homeowner, an older person. Barbara Clapham (97), living with Beth Cook (26), was enthusiastic about the scheme. "All my contemporaries have gone, which is boring. So it's nice to have someone round the place." This scheme ensures that the older person is not segregated by age, or isolated, and that they have some domestic support. It's a win–win situation.

Cohousing is very strong in Denmark and Holland, but only slowly taking off here in the UK. Shared housing arrangements provide for independence within a supportive and age-mixed environment. Participants are usually active in the project, sharing the cooking of some meals, gardening, providing specific professional or practical skills for the community and contributing to the shared governance structure. Members benefit from savings through shared facilities such as laundry, solar panels and heating.

Pioneers agree that it takes time and energy to develop such projects in the UK. Two particular obstacles are negotiating mortgage arrangements that satisfy lenders and finding accessible land for building projects. These are grassroots schemes and some have been started expressly to serve the needs of older people. Older people are not yet well represented in cohousing in the UK, perhaps because of the practical difficulties. In the Netherlands there has been more success, with 200 senior cohousing schemes.[20]

Cohousing in the UK takes various forms. OWCH (Older Women's CoHousing) has just (in 2016) opened its second project in Barnet. In Essex the LoCo Group (London Countryside Housing Group) is developing a project for 23 homes, open to men and women. Members' thinking was influenced by wanting to find a better way than had been available for their parents.[21]

The Threshold Centre in Dorset has been going for some time, and the four residents are all single and over 60. Andrew (68) gardens and cooks and involves himself in other communal activities, as he told the *Guardian Weekend*:

> "I am a co-owner and could not afford to live here without being in a housing association-funded property. I have a share in two acres of garden and grounds, as well as a farmhouse, which are all part of the development, and I have the love and support of people around me, whom I have actively chosen as neighbours."[22]

A much bigger cohousing project is Woodchester Valley, with 73 residential dwellings. This village was built and managed as a retirement village but was bought by the residents, at some expense, after a period of financial turmoil.[23]

In Lilac Grove, Leeds, a cohousing project with 20 homes has been established. And another in Cambridge, called K1, has been set up with 40 homes. These two projects have been supported by the respective city councils, which see them as a potential contribution to housing stock.[24] These are small beginnings for cohousing, but may provide the kind of communities that support older people.

We have not heard of older people being **Property Guardians**, but there is no reason why they should not be. These property guardianships are short-term and affordable rentals of empty properties. And the expansion of informal arrangements, such as renting rooms, also provides ways of sharing costs and increasing networks and social engagement.

One community that embraces many of the features of a wise community is the garden village of New Earswick near York. Maintained by the Joseph Rowntree Trust, the village has schools, a village hall, called a 'Folk Hall', sports facilities, shops and a surgery. It provides opportunities for community involvement and volunteering through the Residents and Community Association. According to the promotional literature, the Trust aims to provide appropriate housing for people throughout their lives.[25]

Bryony (81), a retired teacher, told us how she and her friends talk a great deal about arrangements in old age. She described two advantages of the integrated approach that she observed when on a visit to a former neighbour now living in Earswick:

> "The most positive aspect for me, when we saw round the old-age part of New Earswick, was that the nursery was in the complex where my old

neighbour lived. The residents were encouraged to go in and read to or play with the children. Also, although our neighbour was living on her own in a little house, she subsequently had a stroke. But because of the set-up she could be looked after and nursed in-house."

How do we get there?

These are ambitious visions for the future of homes for age-inclusive communities. How can a community take steps to achieve the age-integrated housing they would like to see locally? In a time of state retreat and austerity, what chances do ambitious plans have?

The retreat of the state provides communities with some opportunities to take up localisation in their development. For example, the Localism Act 2011 provides the rights to enable communities to determine their own shape, including what should be built locally, through processes such as Neighbourhood Planning.

It can be tough to change established ways of seeing and developing housing. Working as a community to do this can be highly positive, but it requires long hours, unlimited dialogue and working against the grain of established practice. A galvanising cause can help to bring people together who are committed to improving their neighbourhood: a recognised need for some facility, a pub, tearoom or shop run by the community, or objections to a developer's plans.

The capacity to explore and encourage new forms of leadership, facilitation and cooperation has to come from local people. Community action means that sometimes it is not the usual people who step forward. Many older people remain activists and have the skills and the ambition to get things done within their communities, as we note in Chapter Fourteen. Whatever the project, it is likely to be enhanced through dialogue that brings together people of all ages, and people not previously experienced in community projects will develop new skills. It is more likely to result in building more houses and addressing the needs of all community members, including the old.[26] New solutions come from facing housing challenges and improving community facilities.

The possibilities are new, exciting, daunting and an alternative to ignoring older people or placing them in segregated housing. They provide opportunities for everyone to use their skills and experiences and to participate in ways that benefit everyone into the future.

What needs to change?

- *Building more houses*: The housing shortage will continue unless the rate of house building increases.
- *Building more suitable houses*: Unless the need for suitable housing for older people is met, the housing shortage will continue. Suitable housing means manageable in terms of finance, support and community. Such housing would suit others in need of accommodation as well. Housing policy needs to attend to all aspects of housing, including wealth and investment generation at the expense of housing. Amending mortgage conditions to make co-housing easier is an example.
- *Listening to older people*: New housing and community development needs to be guided by what older people say they want and need. This will reflect a diversity of wants and needs. Assumptions and ageist views about housing and the ageing population must be challenged.
- *Encouraging community planning for age-integration*: Integrating the older members of the community ensures that neighbourhoods gain the benefits of their experience.

- *Designing communities that are age-inclusive and wise*: Wise development involves and is led by members of the community, regardless of age. For older people this can result in less isolation and loneliness; allow older leadership; and ensure that the small improvements that make big changes benefit everyone.
- *Democratising and localising housing development*: This involves local communities seizing opportunities to develop their own communities, through processes that encourage participation and leadership by older members as much as all other members.

TEN

Who cares?

Care is seen as a problem when it relates to older people. The first response of our interviewees, when asked about the implications for society of an ageing population, was concern about the increasing costs of care. "Huge cost implications", "costs obviously" were typical openers and some people then continued to talk about the increasing burden on the young, and then about the horrors of care homes, including "elder abuse". Although we do not ignore these negative aspects of care, in this chapter we put care of the ageing into perspective and question some of the myths around it, recognising that we need to plan positively for the care of older people both now and in the future.

First of all, what do we mean by 'care'? In practical terms we mean social and medical care, but it is more than that; it is a positive concept encompassing love and respect. It involves reaching out to an individual socially and emotionally as well as looking after them physically. Caring for others is the mark of a civilised society. Sometimes it feels as if this richer meaning of care has been forgotten. Care includes 'care for' but also 'care about'.[1] The person who gives care benefits, as well as the person receiving care.

We all need and receive care when we are children and that is usually taken for granted. People need care and support at any stage of their life, for example when they are ill, and those of us with special needs or disabilities might need care throughout the lifecourse; and as one of our interviewees pointed out, "not all elderly people need care and not all vulnerable people are elderly". However, as this book is about ageing our focus will be on care and support in older age, looking at:

• who is giving care
• types of care and support
• who is paying – some of the myths
• challenges associated with caring
• what needs to change in the care of older people.

Who is giving care?

The pattern of care giving for older people in the UK and elsewhere is complicated, but there are basically three sources of support:

• the unpaid care given by family members and sometimes by neighbours and friends;
• care in the home that is paid for by the individual or by their family or by the local authority;
• care provided in a care or nursing home that is paid for by the individual or by their family or by the local authority.

The voluntary/charity sector, such as Age UK, is also important, providing support and offering comprehensive information for older people and their families as well as undertaking research and campaigning on behalf of older people.

Families offering care

We spoke to Dayo, a Nigerian woman in her late 50s, who saw looking after older people within the family as completely natural:

> "Old age is like growing down after having grown up. We don't take children away from their parents and loved ones regardless of their health issues (and children do have a few). A family can raise three, four or five children, which is about as many elderly parents a couple have, so where does the idea that old people go into care homes come from?"

We like the idea of 'growing down', but in Western societies and increasingly throughout the world there is a tendency for families to be nuclear rather than extended and for a move towards individualistic rather than collectivist values.[2] In a collectivist culture the well-being of the family or community is dominant over the desires of the individual and in such a culture it is the norm for older people to be cared for in the home. However, as Atul Gawande notes, now only about 10% of Europeans over the age of 80 live with their family and even in the East, where collectivist values predominate, the percentage of older people who live alone is rising rapidly.[3] Mita, who is in her 60s, commented on how, despite the maintenance of traditions, social expectations are changing in India to be more like those in the West, with younger people being less likely than they once were to offer older people a home:

> "In a way I think sometimes if there was decent provision for elderly people they might even prefer to be living away from their families as long

> as they saw them regularly. It would give them
> some independence as well. It is just a question of
> money. Individuals can put money away for this.
> One of the reasons I save myself is so that I am
> not dependent on family."

Although in the West we do not generally have older people living in an extended family, families play a big part in their care. In recent censuses, between 13% and 16% of adults report that they are carers; in the 2011 Census this amounted to nearly five million people.[4]

Older people are actually doing much of the caring for other older people, who may be their parents, their partners or their friends. Age UK estimates that there are 1.2 million people over the age of 65 who are undertaking this unpaid care and, of these, nearly 90,000 are over 85, over half in this older group being men.[5] Many older people find themselves juggling with work commitments, care for parents and possibly childcare responsibilities all at the same time – a situation that can induce guilt. Amelia (64), who shares the care of her mother with her sister, was in this position:

> "Then there is also looking after grandchildren. I
> don't want to be committed, but my daughter told
> me that my granddaughter who is four is going
> straight into school and will have to go to an after
> school-club. I said maybe we could help out!"

For the many older people who live alone (mainly women) family care is typically given by their children (mainly daughters or daughters-in-law). It is difficult to be sure of the exact amount of unpaid care, as it may be under-reported, but it is mainly done by women, most often in the 45–64 age group.[6] The importance of close family in caring begs the question of who will support the growing proportion of older people who do not have children, as well as highlighting how the care of older people is disproportionally undertaken by women. It also raises the question of who cares for the carers. These figures show that families actually do a great deal of caring for their older members, despite the apparent perception of the callousness of families in the West. Is this an example of a myth about care and ageing?

Paid care in the home

Paid-for care administered through local authority adult care services in England is subject to a means test and about 4% of older people are eligible, while another 4% pay for their own care.[7] In contrast, 58% of older people participating in a 2008 study reported that they had no help and 34% reported that they had informal help from family, neighbours and friends.[8]

Those who qualify to receive care from the local authority may get only one 15-minute visit a day, although this is certainly not recommended.[9] With these time restraints made worse by cuts in local authority funding, not all carers can offer totally appropriate care. There is also the issue of carers' training and education. For example, in the case of Dorothy (89), one of the authors witnessed her carer continually addressing her inappropriately as 'my little sweetie' and rubbing her face, saying 'look at your lovely chubby cheeks', infantilising the person being cared for. The carer herself was aged 64.

What about care homes?

When we asked people to estimate what proportion of older people were in care homes the guesses were often around 50%. Is our common over-estimate another example of a myth about ageing? In fact only 3–4% of the over-65s and 13% of people over 85 are in care homes and the proportion entering care homes does not appear to be rising.[10] Popular media coverage would have us believe that many of us inevitably end our lives in care homes, but this is just not the case and Richard, who is in his 70s, commented:

> "Not everyone needs long-term care. The incidence in reality is lower than perception. Do governments suggest it is a problem in order to get people to squirrel money away to provide for themselves?"

There is a blurred distinction between residential care homes and nursing homes. In England, all are now known as 'care homes', with the majority being residential and not offering nursing. On the whole, a small proportion of people enter either type of home towards the end of their life and the average stay is relatively short; in England only 27% of residents live for three years or more in care homes,[11] and the average stay in a nursing home is about five months.[12]

There are many fine care homes, where individuals are treated with respect and thoughtfulness as well as having their physical needs attended to. Alice, an agency care worker who is in her 60s, showed just this when offering us examples from her work, one of which follows.

> "There was a bell ringing so I trotted along to Room One, switched the bell off at the wall and found that Mr Wilson had spilt his tea all over the floor. What patients often don't realise is just what a pleasure it is to help. If he hadn't spilt his tea, I wouldn't be needed – I wouldn't have the opportunity to give – and as I get older myself and have days when I haven't the energy to do more than look after myself, I appreciate more and more just what a treat it is to help other people."

It is good to remember that there are stories from carers like this to put alongside the media's frightening stories of neglect. In many cases the situation is neither neglect nor stimulation to live as good a life as possible. As Jane (71) commented: "In old people's homes, people have low expectations and sit there." A study of old people in residential homes in Ireland found that the quality of life was better where individuals had their own rooms, felt empowered to make their own decisions about the shape of their day rather than being subject to institutional 'rules' and were living in a 'person centred' environment.[13] We discussed some of these issues relating to the older person's quality of life in the previous chapter. Some of our interviewees were concerned not to be subjected to a rigid regime and uniform treatment. For example, Kate (65) said she hoped for

> "quality residential care which is available for all, not just those who can afford to pay a lot for it; residential care which does not work on heteronormative stereotypes; the opportunity to mix with people of similar interests/life experience when I'm not able to manage that for myself."

What type of care and support?

As people age they are likely to need more care, both medical and social, and their needs may change and increase. Assessing whether a person can live independently or whether they need assistance is difficult. Different results come out of different surveys, so that there is no 'right' answer to exactly how many people need what type of care.[14] Understandably, older people may be somewhat resistant to the idea that they need help, particularly when most care comes under the heading of personal care. Such care includes help with bathing and dressing, preparing meals, care of the home, shopping and cleaning, support with telephoning and taking medicine. But care is not just about dealing with physical matters. Support that focuses on social and emotional needs can be just as important. Having good personal relationships with family and others; maintaining interest in the community; having social contact and leisure activities all help to delay the need for physical assistance and delay the onset of health problems.[15, 16] Being able to benefit others and feel that you are offering something back to society also improves well-being and keeps people active, helping to avoid the need for medical intervention. Pauline, an ex-GP in her 70s whom we interviewed, gave an example:

> "Many charities are very dependent on the retired population. Our local church runs a weekly lunch club which is basically managed by pensioners for local people, including transport when needed. The meal is supplied by a local trust which trains people with learning difficulties to fit them for paid employment. Using the church's kitchen they prepare, serve and clear up the meal. The lunchers enjoy the meal and company and chat to the young people, with benefit to both."

Through such local bonds and the existence of classes such as those provided by U3A or the Workers' Educational Association, older people have opportunities to keep on growing and learning. In these ways we can care for older people, value them and enhance their well-being, and their physical health, postponing the need for more extensive support.

Unfortunately, social contact is often restricted or prevented by lack of transport, in particular the reduction or removal of bus services, especially in rural areas. The importance of this was picked up by several of our interviewees. Cutting back on care and support, including public transport that enables older people to take part in the community and have an active social life, is likely to be counterproductive.

Typically, people prefer to remain in their own home for as long as possible, which is the preferred option not only of individuals and their families but also of the state.[17] However, moving into residential care may become inevitable for the minority who simply are not able to care for themselves, even with support in their home. Over half of those who move into residential homes are suffering from some form of cognitive decline that makes it necessary for them to have constant support on hand. We will look further at dementia and the way that it is handled in the next chapter.

For some older people, care will come from a combination of sources, depending on their circumstances and ability to pay: the family, the state or a private carer and a care home. One of our interviewees, Miriam, who is in her late 60s, along with her husband, helped to support her mother-in-law to stay in her own home for several years after she was widowed. Their regular support was supplemented by a paid-for carer. Eventually, well into her 90s, the mother-in-law's mental condition deteriorated and she went into a care home, where family support continued in the form of regular visits.

Who pays for care?

Most care is needed in the final years of life and, as people live longer, they are also more likely to have more than one chronic condition and therefore to need more medical as well as social care. No one can accurately predict how much the increased costs will be, but the main driver of costs is thought to be advances in medicine and the increase in types of treatment available. Simply blaming the increase in health costs on a single cause – the ageing population – turns out to be another potential myth.[18]

The question of who pays for the growing costs implicit in the care of the ageing population is one that worried our interviewees. Some of the darker implications that they saw were the growing resentment of older people by the young. Lorna (59) told us:

> "When I was growing up, the older generation were the war winners so it was unthinkable to turn on them (at least openly) but now that taboo is well broken although I was still shocked the first time I heard vocal opposition to the baby boomers – 'they've had their time and now it's ours'."

How much of the costs of care should be paid by the individual and how much funded by taxpayers through the state is a fundamental question. As we have seen, those who have enough money generally pay their own costs, and they benefit from that in having more choice and a potentially better standard of care. On the other hand, there are issues of equity. When we spoke to Richard, in his early 70s, he commented on his mother-in-law's situation:

> "Who should provide? Should people be penalised or rewarded for being profligate or for saving? Some people cannot contribute, of course. There is a problem in society of envy and resentment. When my mother-in-law was in a home in a less-than-affluent area she was the only one who was self-funded. The people who really resented her paying were those who owned the home. They thought it was unjust, but she was in a situation to pay. They thought that as the state was paying for all the rest why did the state not pay for her?"

Whether the state or the individual and their family should pay for care at home or in a residential or nursing home is a difficult question and applies internationally. In the case of England, social care is means tested and medical care is provided free through the NHS. But what actually counts as medical care and what counts as social care? At present, all personal care is considered social care, so that, for example, in a fairly typical care-home case quoted to us:

> "A woman in her 90s was completely unable to look after herself as she was deeply cognitively impaired with dementia. In addition she was unable to bear her own weight, unable to feed herself, certainly not wash or dress herself, was doubly incontinent and had skin breakdowns, chronic kidney problems and frequent chest infections and still was classified as needing social rather than medical care."

Medical care is very strictly defined, and seen as an intervention that requires the regular attention of a qualified practitioner, not just regular visits from the district nurse backed up by care with bathing and washing, feeding and so on. Where an individual needs this type of social care and has assets they are expected to pay their own costs, whether they are looked after at home or in a care or nursing home, until their savings, including the value realised from the sale of their house, have been reduced to a specified sum. At the time of writing the introduction of a cap on the total amount that an individual should pay towards their care has been put on hold. The system that governs the financing of the care of older people is so complex that it provides fertile ground for the growth of myths, misinformation and Kafkaesque scenarios of tracking down who is responsible for what. It is also ever changing, so that anyone faced with financing care should check the current details through an organisation like Age UK.

There has been a move towards personal care budgets in England. Where someone is eligible for local authority support they can now choose to receive a direct payment of the amount that the local authority would spend on their care and decide how to spend it themselves. This enhances choice, but there are disadvantages. If the person chooses not to use an agency, which employs and pays the carers, the person themselves has to become an employer, with all the legal and moral obligations that this implies. There are other potential difficulties. Bryony, who is in her 80s, commented on the circumstances of a friend:

> "Personal budgets with which older people can purchase their own care are not the answer for everyone, as some would find the energy and work involved too much. I recently spent a few days with an old friend who had had a stroke. She had speech but no mobility except for one arm. She had an electric wheelchair for the house and everything was at the right height for this but her whole day was spent organising her own care. All her energy was directed towards keeping this degree of independence and anyone staying or calling was organised into fulfilling this end. Her son next door was called on to fill any gaps in her care."

Fair funding of the care and support of older people is a huge challenge for policy and practice, raising the most basic questions about the values of our society. In times when a neoliberal agenda predominates, it is likely that more and more responsibility will be placed in the hands of individuals and their families and the market will dominate in the provision of paid care. In these circumstances the provision of care for older people will be patchy, with better care for those who can afford it and lack of equity in provision overall.

What needs to change?

Look at care differently

At present it seems that we look only at the negatives in relation to the care of the ageing population. There are continued crises and regular news stories about the growing 'burden' of the old. And yet there are many positives, including the amount of care given by older people to other older people and the fulfilment to be gained helping other people. The huge contribution of care by families is heartening, and continuing involvement in the community means that older people maintain their health and independence for longer.

We started this chapter by commenting that the care of older people is often seen as a problem; but (hopefully) we will all be older people some day, and older people are not a separate species that can be disregarded, ignored or just looked after as cheaply as possible. There are all sorts of ways in which we can ensure that older people are integrated into the community so that they remain vital and involved as long as possible. We have seen how social involvement fends off the physical problems of old age. Pedro (55) called for "some fundamental social/cultural changes in attitude (ultimately manifest in economic change)", and others felt that there is a need to look for a fresh approach. Lorna (59) said:

> "It would be nice to think of this as an opportunity – our cohort leading the charge into a new and better time for older people because how we manage ourselves as older people will in time get picked up as future models for government help

and projects – such as job shares between old and young, skill swaps, housing projects etc."

There is a feeling that the children of the 1960s and later will demand more as they age and will complain when they are treated inappropriately. Bernadette (66), who is an accomplished artist, gave an example of such treatment:

> "I went to an 'Imaginative Art' workshop at my local Age UK centre. I met the tutor, who said we wouldn't be painting but working in 3D. I was excited about that as I had not created much sculpture. She said she was thinking of making hats with scrunched up pieces of tissue paper so that older people could wear them at a sing-song evening!"

Sort out the complexity

When we spoke to Miriam (69) she commented on just how difficult it is to access a range of services:

> "When people need support in older age there should be an integrated service that snaps into place. It would be great if there was one place you could contact and be told exactly what you should do next and what you are entitled to."

The difficulty of identifying what is social care and may have to be paid for and what is free medical care, supplied by the NHS, is a particular area of potential confusion, not just for the older person and their family, but also for those working in the system. For example, at present there are often delays in the discharge of an older person from hospital when a package of care is needed. Reform in this area would be cost saving and efficient for everyone concerned. Margaret (71) suggested that "We also need recuperation centres so that elderly patients with mobility issues can be moved out of the main hospitals and given good physiotherapy so they can return to their homes" rather than being placed unnecessarily in residential homes.

Although the Care Act 2014 in England aims to bring together health and social services, the system remains complex and difficult to navigate.

Another aspect of complexity is the need to access technology, as we recognised in our discussions about older consumers (see Chapter Five). Jane (71), who works in the field of care and social services, suggested that what older people need is

> "advocacy and support to find a way through systems that one might need as one gets older. I really think that life is getting more complicated and more difficult to cope with and old people need more help as a result. I am sure that life was simpler for my parents. They used to pay bills with wodges of money and walked to places like the coal merchant to pay them. Now so much is online."

Treat the individual as a person, not a symptom

Another problem with the system is that individuals are not seen as a whole person, but as someone presenting with a specific symptom that needs treating. Many older people will have complex needs arising from a number of different health problems, as well as needing social care. Pauline, an ex-GP aged 74, explained: "medical training does not include adequate training for treatment of the elderly where they are often faced with multiple pathologies. It is too easy for an orthopaedic surgeon to know very little about cardiac problems in the fractured-hip lady." She went on to comment:

> "Changes in management of the provisions for the elderly could vastly improve their well-being. For example, if GPs were able to be more readily available and, with their nurses, had a properly organised system of review of all their patients on medication, there would be better management and problems could be spotted and dealt with earlier."

Provide for those without family support

So much care of older people is undertaken by family. What if the family does not want to be involved, is too far away or is non-existent? For a variety of reasons, many people do not have children and a proportion of older people, particularly men, report that they are isolated or lonely. This is a growing issue, as the population of older men is growing faster than the population of older women, who are in any case more likely to have good social contacts and to seek medical advice more readily.[19] As the number of older men grows it is important that their access to social and medical support is monitored and that provision is made for their interests, as well as ensuring that there are networks to monitor the needs of all older people without immediate family.

Dignity and diversity in care homes

There is a challenge here in providing care of a universally high quality, and also providing care homes that offer differentiated types of care suiting the variety of needs of a diverse older population, as we saw in the previous chapter.

Although people may typically live in care homes for only a relatively short time, 'residential care settings are not places to die, they are places in which to live and live well'.[20]

Prioritise planning

In order to implement all these changes we need to engage in holistic planning. A recent report by an independent commission investigating the provision of urgent care for old people basically concluded that we need to be proactive in planning for the care of older members of our society, not reactive as we are at present.[21] Specifically in relation to the care and support of older people, a conference on 'The Future of Ageing in the UK' put as society's first two priorities:

1. Health must find a way to be more responsive and preventative.
2. Government must make progress in delivering a long term settlement to pay for social care.[22]

Finally

We have seen through this chapter that there are misconceptions and myths about older people, such as an under-estimation of the role that families (including older people themselves) actually play in looking after their older members. Above all, we stress that older people are not separate from the rest of society and that it is only a matter of time before any of us might need care. While there are certainly challenges relating to care for older people there is actually both good news and there is the potential for fresh and exciting ways of approaching care for all of us as we age. We need to wake up and plan ahead for a society that is inclusive and values all its members.

ELEVEN

The dark side

There is no denying that ageing brings with it physical and possibly mental deterioration, the increased likelihood of chronic illness and eventual death, but, despite what are seen as the problems of older age, a recent survey indicates that older people all report higher levels of happiness and life satisfaction than people in their middle years.[1]

Our preferred view of ageing, explained in Chapter Three, is of a continuous lifecourse where, at any age, individuals might face the most difficult aspects of life, such as bereavement or ill-health. Throughout this book we take a new look at ageing for the current and future generations, who, compared to previous generations, will live longer, have better health and will not accept the staid and outdated stereotypes that have in the past accrued to old age. How can and will the new generations of older people understand and handle the challenges that are more likely to come with age?

This chapter is structured around the major concerns about older age identified by our interviewees: first, their sense of mortality, often brought on by their own illness or the illness or death of someone close to them; then the related fear of having to live with illness or frailty and being dependent on others, with the possible onset of dementia being a particular concern. In addition, people spoke of the potential for depression in older age, perhaps as a result of or perhaps caused by loneliness. There was awareness that all the difficulties that might darken the last stages of life would be made worse by poverty. The chapter ends with insights from the narratives about what can be good and positive in addressing the darker side of old age, reviewing what we have learned and looking at how things should change.

Facing the prospect of death

The 20th-century philosopher and writer Albert Camus wrote in the margins of one of his notebooks: 'Come to terms with death. Thereafter anything is possible.'[2] That may be true, but coming to terms with death is not simple, particularly as death is something of a taboo subject. Wanda, a bereavement counsellor in her 60s, reflecting on her experience working in the UK, felt that "As a society we need to break through the taboo of denial of death and find the courage to prepare ourselves for this inevitable event."

For most of us, it is relatively easy to avoid thinking about death. It is generally experienced on the margins of social life, with most deaths in developed countries occurring in institutions, mainly in hospitals rather than at home, although the majority express a preference for dying at home.[3] Reluctance to contemplate death extends to writing a will; only 35% of adults have done this, while only 5% have set out how they would like to be cared for at the end of their life.[4] Death may be regarded very differently in different cultures and moderated by religious practices, but in Western societies, even among the very old, there is a tendency to push thoughts of death aside. David Winter, in his 80s and ex-head of BBC religious broadcasting, has found that death does not dominate the thinking of older people, who see it as happening to others. He commented that, of all the books he had written, the one on death, although it sold better than the others, was the only book he had never been asked to talk about in public.[5] It is perhaps not surprising that some of our interviewees did not even mention death or did not want to talk about it. Tom (62), who has cancer, stated:

> "You don't want to think about death, just don't want to be there. Life is an enjoyable experience, you think about what and who you are leaving behind. At the moment I am finding all these things fairly easy to ignore, I don't want to think about them. There is probably a time when you do plan your funeral, but not yet. Ask me again when I am 85."

Others who mentioned death were those who had recovered from serious illnesses or experienced the death or illness of someone very close to them, acting as a reminder of mortality. This was true of Mita, who is in her mid-60s.

> "I had breast cancer, and fortunately for me it was detected very early. That is a wake-up call. It's quite scary. You don't know how long you have. It's made me look at life differently. I am thankful to be OK and live the time I have."

Our interviewees ranged in age from the mid-50s to the late 80s and there appeared to be a progression in their acceptance of death as they got older. Madge put this well:

> "To paraphrase what the American poet George Oppen said to Paul Auster about old age, 'What a strange thing to happen to a little [girl]'. Don't we all start off thinking we're immortal or that the inevitability (if we're lucky) of becoming old or

physically frail is meant for other people? ... it's only now that I think increasingly about mortality, about the fragility and comparative brevity of our lives, and that I read the obituaries in the paper first, before even doing the crossword."

And Richard, in his early 70s, stated that "You are now 80% through your life and that is just factual recognition. It does not prey on my mind, but it is there to a greater extent than it was."

Those who were still in their 50s and had experienced the death of someone close tended to be more distanced in their thoughts of death. Samantha, in her 50s, had learned from her personal experiences and losses through the deaths of those close to her, but was applying the lessons to her current life rather than thinking about her own death:

"I was 25 when my father died, 39 when my mother died and 40 when my husband died and the gift I feel they have given me is my zest for life. I never forget how fragile life is, which gives you an urgency about life to try and do as much as you can while and when you can and enjoy life ... People are the most important thing and the relationships you have with them and the memories you make with them and I try and make as many memories as possible now."

Older interviewees saw death as applying more directly to them. Emma, who is in her 70s, and who has faced serious illness in both herself and her husband, commented: "time is passing and who knows what is in store? How many more books am I going to be able to read? Things are finite." Maureen (85) similarly thought: "I do have a sense of time running out, but not fast. When people announce stuff about the High Speed trains being ready in 2030 or 2040 that's when I think, 'but I won't be there'."

Although some of the interviewees talked about death, on the whole they were not dwelling on it or thinking about it deeply, although a few expressed a feeling of curiosity about their own death.

For most people there is a final period of life when decline towards death occurs. Obviously there is no single pattern, and even with knowledge that an illness is terminal it is impossible to estimate the how long an individual will live. Atul Gawande, the 2015 Reith lecturer, a doctor with vast experience of end of life, comments that even where patients and their families had known for some time that they had a terminal condition 'they – along with their families and doctors – were unprepared for the final stage'. Also, even though doctors and patients are having more conversations about what is wanted at the end of life, 'The problem is that's way too late'.[6] Even gerontologists and those working in medicine have tended not to discuss all the social implications of death until relatively recently,[7] but advocacy by groups like Age UK is moving us towards empowerment of the dying, ensuring that, where possible, the individual remains in control and maintains dignity to the last.

The advice is therefore that we should prepare. Only one interviewee, Bernadette (66), seemed to have taken this advice to heart:

> "The issue of dying is one I am particularly interested in. We need to address this individually and as a society, but maybe this issue is for your next book. We must find a way to make death less of a taboo subject and develop clear and positive language to talk about dying and our own death. So in providing support for older people we need to help them face death and have a comfortable

THE NEW AGE OF AGEING

dying with dignity and humanity. More hospices
would be good, and more choice."

She is right that the topic of death is not the focus of this
book, and the many issues involved in a measured discussion
of death are of immense importance, among them: palliative
care; the importance of hospices; making a will and issues
of power of attorney; living wills; the 'good' death, assisted
death and the diversity of the ways in which death is regarded
in different cultures. They require at least a whole book to
be considered fully.

Living with illness

A proportion of older people live with a limiting long-
standing illness, estimated at 40% of all people aged over
65 and two-thirds of people over 85 in the UK,[8] but many
people will find ways of adapting to living with chronic
conditions and maintaining a good quality of life, and this
was true of many of our interviewees. Tom (62) is living
with cancer:

"I have been pulled up a bit by what has happened.
There is a bit of denial there. Frequent visits to the
hospital remind you but I just don't feel it. I can
contribute at home and at work. I don't worry
about it. All my peers – we never talk about it, we
just think about doing the next thing."

It is understandable that the older interviewees were much
more aware of their own frailties, but our experience was
that, unlike Gill Pharoah, quoted at the start of the book,
they were generally positive and resilient in the face of illness
and injury. Elizabeth, now in her late 80s, commented that
she first became aware of being old

"about seven years ago in my early 80s. My expectations after each fracture were that I would just get better and get on with life and manage, but I needed a good deal more care than I thought."

Ralph (82) equally showed resilience when faced with a variety of age-related problems, stating that he was playing tennis twice a week, usually two or three sets, but noticing "stamina – less, speed – less, hand–eye coordination goes sometimes resulting in more 'air' shots, slight hearing loss, less energy", and commenting that he had had a minor stroke a year before.

Several of those who were younger recounted the experience of falls or fractures that made them aware of what life might be like when older and possibly permanently incapacitated. Bernadette, in her mid-60s, had this experience after a bad break of her wrist:

"It was awful. I hated asking for help, I hated not being mobile. I wanted to be independent. I imagined that this is what it might be like to be older. I hated it…. It was madly frustrating. This incident shook me, as I have always been fit and healthy and I have never had any condition that affected my mobility. So I had a glimpse of what it would be like if I became in any way infirm. I didn't like it."

That fear of dependence was one that affected people with regard to partners and children. Tilda (89) felt this strongly:

"I hope I'm not being a nuisance, being a drag. I feel that however well-meaning the intentions, looking after a parent who is deteriorating, especially mentally, becomes a huge burden. I don't want to be thought of that way and seeing what you were being obliterated. Better to be in impersonal surroundings than a burden. I feel that's the right way to feel about it. It's not good for my children to get too involved. My children are getting towards retirement and I don't want them to spend retirement looking after me."

There was also the fear and concern that people felt for their partners, particularly when illness was potentially life threatening. Emma (71) stated:

"I don't worry about my own health, but J's [husband] health I worry about. The Parkinson's will get worse. I don't think I am very patient. I made a decision that I was not going to ruin the present by worrying about the future. The last few months [when her husband has had cancer of the colon] has given me a taste of what illness is like. I see some short-comings in myself. J is extremely good about not worrying about the future."

Although most of our interviewees either were still healthy or had adapted to living successfully with illnesses, we appreciate that illness will reach a point where it dominates the life of an individual and their partner or other close relatives. As discussed earlier in the chapter, there comes a time towards the end of life when illnesses reach a final stage and when attention may finally turn to planning for a good death.

Dementia and fear of dementia

A fear of succumbing to dementia is probably the most common concern of individuals as they get older, now exceeding the fear of cancer.[9] Certainly our interviewees were concerned about it. Ruth, who is only in her early 60s, expressed how she feared dementia more than death:

> "I'd like a good death, and a healthy life but not necessarily a long one. My Mum died aged 78 and didn't live long enough to develop dementia, as my maternal aunts have done, later in life. I want to go before dementia or too many other limiting medical problems set in. I hope I'm brave and able enough to take my own life, when the time is right."

There is also anxiety that dementia might affect someone close, who will then need increasing levels of support. Although there is a fear of the disease there is growing knowledge and understanding of its progress and manifestations, through the activities of associated charities and through the cinema and books, such as the films *Still Alice* and *Away from Her* and Elizabeth Healey's award-winning novel *Elizabeth is missing*.

It is estimated that there are over 800,000 people with dementia in the UK, approximately 1 in 14 of people aged over 65.[10] As the likelihood of having dementia increases with age, the worst-case scenario is that there will be an increase of over 150%, to more than two million, by 2051.[11] However, there is evidence that in the more developed countries the rate is starting to fall with better general and cardio-vascular health. There are also regular announcements about the development of new drugs that will in time alleviate or even cure some forms of dementia; for example the discovery in 2015 of drugs already available that show potential for delaying the progress of Alzheimer's might 'change the disease into something completely different and infinitely more acceptable to society'.[12] Despite the importance of this type of research, we spend less on dementia research than we do on other life-threatening diseases such as cardiovascular disease and cancer. Even though advances are being made, for the long-term benefit of individuals, families and communities it is vital that government makes it a priority to put more funds into research in this area.[13]

For those who have dementia, and for their families, there are important advances in educating the wider public and making cities and communities more dementia friendly; for example, a dementia training programme for student hairdressers, or a drive to improve banking services for people with dementia.[14] There was even a G8 summit on dementia in 2013, as all countries are facing the same issues. As we indicated in the last chapter, policies to join up social and medical care might prove both cost-effective and appropriate for older people, particularly those with dementia, many of whom could be cared for for longer in their own homes with suitable support, rather than occupying a hospital or care-home bed.

Dementia is often an important factor in the decision to move from living with support in the community to living in a care home. Approximately 80% of those in care homes in England have some form of dementia or severe memory loss.[15] Marianne, one of the authors of this book, has personal experience of supporting a relative with dementia, first in her own home and later in a care home. Here are some brief extracts from what was recorded over the four years in the care home.

> During the time she has been there M has been getting gradually more confused. Her confusion takes the form of merging past and present so that

themes from the past are peopled in the present by a cast that includes her mother, her husband (who died several years ago) and the carers and fellow residents of the care home. However, when it comes to everyday things such as clothes, food and sleep, she is quite normal.

People with dementia are often living in a past or a different sort of present that is totally real to them and I was first of all advised to correct rather than collude and go along with her stories but later I changed my mind. I enjoyed talking to M about her past and learnt that it was only distressing to M if I continued to insist on the truth, for example, that individuals she clearly saw in hallucinations were no longer alive.

As time went on physical problems hastened the progress of the dementia.

M has been in hospital for about five weeks and was discharged about four weeks ago. She had a fall and broke a bone in her pelvis and had to be able to bear weight and walk a few steps before she could go back to the care home. Now she is in better shape physically than she was before she went in, but her mental state is gradually deteriorating. She is becoming more challenging in her behaviour and refusing to co-operate with the care assistants about virtually everything; taking pills; going to the dining room; having her hair done.

However dire the circumstances, M retained her basic personality and there were occasional moments of clarity and insight as well as good natured humour that provided comfort and happiness. Not long before she died there was a lovely moment when she said to me that the ceiling was nothing special, but (and here she became conspiratorial) it did keep the rain off you know.

She knew that she recognised me (she does not always now) and that I was her daughter-in -law, but she was surprised that I was married to her son and had to be reminded who he was. At one point she said I was just like that nice girl who comes to visit her!

Of course Marianne was that 'nice girl'. Her mother-in-law died at 99, but the experiences of another author of this book, Eileen, were very different as they were of early-onset dementia in her family, and the repercussions of this were felt throughout her adult life:

"My Mum died when she was 69. I was 30. She had been ill for a very long time, probably from around the time I was a small child. What seemed to be depression developed over the years to withdrawal till she didn't really communicate with anyone at all, even my Dad. The awful thing was that I didn't know what to do or how to support her. We didn't talk about it much as a family and the GP just put her on tranquillisers and probably anti-depressants. When I was about 22 she had ECT [electro-convulsive therapy] and was in hospital for a few weeks. After that she seemed much more withdrawn. It was heart-breaking. When I was 40, ten years after my mother's death, I did see a therapist and talked for the first time about what it all meant to me. I cried and cried. It was the start of my mourning."

When her two older sisters suffered the same illness and died at similar ages, Eileen needed "therapy to make sense of it" and stated that "I could have done with support earlier and came to understand the value of talking through one's feelings with very expert therapists".

Clearly, the dark side of the process of growing older can be extremely challenging and stressful for the individual and those closest to them.

Loneliness and depression

Although more women than men live alone, women tend to be better at keeping in touch with family and friends, they are more likely to take part in social activities and to look after their health and are less likely than men to say that they feel lonely.[16] Although the differences in life expectancy are narrowing, at present 5% more women than men aged 65–79 live alone. In the older age group of over-80s the differential is nearer 20%, with 60.4% of women against nearly 40% of men living alone.[17] Inevitably, most of us will experience some loneliness as we grow older as partners and friends die. People who might be good companions for holidays or trips may no longer be available, through death or ill-health. Kate (65) identified how the loneliness brought about by the death of a partner might be compounded by an inevitable change in domestic circumstances. She commented on how difficult it was:

> "Observing my parents' experience of having to leave their own home, and accept that they couldn't cope on their own any more. Also observing my mother's experience of becoming widowed and having to come to terms with living in an unfamiliar place at the same time as grieving for my father."

Deirdre, who is in her 50s, was also aware of a parent's growing loneliness as she inevitably lost her friends: "My mother is 82 and still working as a lawyer two days a week, but her friends are dying, it is very sad. Loneliness and isolation is a challenge." Wanda's experience as a bereavement counsellor was that

> "When working with the bereaved a common factor that emerged was that those who had experienced a fulfilling marriage/relationship generally found it easier to move on, their memories being good, with little bitterness or recrimination. Those who had endured an unhappy relationship often found it harder to move forward, their self-esteem having been shattered, sometimes resulting in temporary loss of the will to live."

Even for those with good memories, the death of someone with whom you have shared your life is an enormous loss, akin to losing part of yourself. Intense grieving tends to last more than a year. Edith, now in her 60s, who also worked as a bereavement counsellor, said:

> "In our organisation we talked with people for at least two years, once a week for an hour. What was important about this experience for the bereaved person was they could talk, over and over again, about things that were important to them. They realised that their friends and relatives would get fed up with hearing about the same old issues. Not many people know how to respond to people who have suffered a loss and often it is the bereaved person who has to cope with other people's issues as well as their own."

In addition, many older people are cared for by their partner and lose the benefit of that care when they are gone. With no partner, there are practical problems in older age. Ruth (65) realised this when:

> "I had a few weeks of ill-health at the end of last year, and did feel quite vulnerable, because of living alone and having few close family members close by. Inevitably, there will be increasing numbers of episodes of illness/hospital appointments and I will need to deal with these alone, or make a huge effort to ask for help, which I'm not good at."

Bryony (81) stressed that there was "an overlap with depression in old age as life inevitably diminishes". Loneliness and possible resulting depression may be experienced by anyone as they age, particularly if they are geographically isolated – for example, living in rural settings where public transport is limited. Not everyone has a family who will support them. In such cases befriending organisations within the local community such as The Campaign to End Loneliness can help to alleviate problems or, alternatively, a national initiative such as Esther Rantzen's Silver Line. Maintaining a role in the local community and keeping contact with others is a vital part of maintaining mental and physical health for longer,[18] and in England local councils recognise the need to work at three levels – strategic, through local communities and one-to-one – to alleviate loneliness.[19]

Ageing in poverty

Much is made of how older people are financially better off than the young, but in a society where there is an increasing divide between the haves and the have-nots, a substantial proportion of older people (65+) in the UK are living below the poverty line. Of these it is estimated that 900,000 are in severe poverty.[20] In the UK, the state pension is relatively low compared with the rest of Europe, at roughly 30% of occupational earnings as compared with 50% for Europe overall.[21] For the better-off, this shortfall is made up by private pensions, but those without that cushion are having a hard time. Older people with limited incomes are reported to find it tough and emotionally draining to make the enormous efforts necessary to manage, making sacrifices such as having no outings or holidays, cutting back on heating and energy costs. Those who are worst off financially are suffering poor health and mobility, living in a rural area with limited or no public transport and have few social networks.[22] Old age brings challenges and difficulties that are considerably worsened where people are living in poverty.

Facing up to the challenges

So, how do we deal with the more challenging aspects of growing older? Most people and most of those we spoke to seem to 'park' serious contemplation of their own deaths or the death of loved ones, although for the older interviewees and those who had experienced a life-threatening illness this was less true. Ralph (82) recognised that with increasing old age there may be acceptance that the end of life is nearing: "Yes I think about death, what kind of death I'm going to have, that's a matter of concern. I used to be more anxious about it. My question is – is one less anxious and more ready to go?"

Contemplating the possibility of the death of his partner, Jack (72) felt that for himself "grief could be mitigated by transferring the deeply felt emotions to positive thoughts towards his children and grandchildren".

A brush with the possibility of an early death had made Mary, now 71, determined to live life to the full, and her resolve is typical of the positive approach to life, illness, loneliness and ageing that was taken by many of those we spoke to.

> "Having had bone cancer in my mid-30s and hearing that my life chances were 50/50 I thought I would not live to see my older years, let alone reach pension age. I felt I had been cheated of life. I think this concentrated my mind. I realised that our lifetime is precious and, as I lived alone, I decided to get on and explore life as much as possible. I joined evening classes for different subjects and managed to go on some holidays as I had not been able to for several years. Later, when I worked abroad I still took every opportunity to explore and meet people to add depth to everything I did. I didn't always get it right and could put myself in difficult situations but I wonder if I would have done all these things if I had not had setbacks. It is a celebration to reach 65+ years."

We seem to have an ability to adjust to our new circumstances as we age and learn to deal with the various problems that arise. So, Elizabeth (89) was able to give the advice: "Make the best of everything – find lots of 'bests' to relish", and gave the example of being taken out in her wheelchair. She added, "count your blessings a lot, remind yourself which bits are lucky, like the success of a cataract operation". She was also maintaining her interests and hobby of crafts involving wool: spinning, natural dyeing, weaving, knitting and then selling at local craft and county shows.

Others also had good advice. Pauline (74), an ex-GP, drew upon her experience to offer the following pointers to us as we age:

- Don't stop and don't feel sorry for yourself.
- Keep as fit as possible and take medication prescribed and as directed. If it does not suit you go back to the doctor. No crystal balls.
- If married or in a partnership, try to have interests of your own that will continue when you are alone. Too many couples do everything together and are then lost as well as grieving.
- Keep up with family and friends – use telephone, texting, Skyping and even writing.
- Continue your normal hobbies but also start some new interests.
- Arrange your business and give someone you trust Power of Attorney that can be activated when needed.

There are unexpected positives even when one is faced with the sudden discovery of a life-threatening illness. Tom (62) reflected that

> "I have found that you start to strengthen your important relationships and that has been brilliant. You make more time to talk to people who you are fond of. Where this comes from is the realisation that it is not going to go on for a lot of time. I am finding it enjoyable and I know that the efforts have to come from me.
>
> "All of that has made me a more considerate person to everyone's good. It adds a dimension. The great thing about it is that nothing irritates me now. I think, just don't go there, it is not worth it. I don't think about people being inconsiderate and I see good in it all."

Most of us don't want to address the full reality of our deaths until the end of life, and perhaps not even then, but as we age we see that our time is limited and our physical resources are diminishing and we adjust to the situation, seeing what is really important in our lives and what we cherish. The experience of losing a loved one, an inevitable part of ageing, may have the same impact. Wanda reflected on her long experience as a bereavement counsellor:

> "Loss enables us to question our values, reappraise and appreciate family, friends and achievements, to come to terms with ourselves and our own needs.
>
> Loss can be a turning point. Therefore it is important that we create positive realities rather than negative thoughts for the future that we have been afforded."

For those who care for older people, including those with dementia, there are compensations and moments of enlightenment. Alice, a carer, described the satisfaction she obtained even from cleaning up people who were incontinent and making them comfortable again. She also described how worthwhile it was to be able to spend time talking to people with dementia:

> "I just love looking into people's eyes and seeing the real person and responding to that – agreeing when agreement is required, trying to make my responses as appropriate as I can even though I sometimes don't know what she's talking about, being playful, finding little ways to make her feel that I'm on her side and that she is liked and loved and understood. This is a game that makes sense to me because it is so worthwhile."

What have we learned about 'the dark side'?

It seems that as individuals we adjust to the challenges of age as we age and our perspectives change. Our older interviewees showed how this adjustment is possible and they also showed fortitude and resilience in their attitudes to life. It seems that our understanding of old age changes: for example, interviewees in their 50s talked about being old once they were 70, but those past 70 or even 80 did not see themselves as old yet.

Research findings bear out the importance of being part of communities as we age. It is clear that it is important to remain in touch with people, to follow hobbies and interests and to continue to be part of social networks in order to maintain physical and mental health as long as possible.

The state has a particular responsibility to look after those who have not had the opportunity to amass savings and contribute to a private pension and who may find themselves without sufficient means to enjoy a reasonable standard of life as they age. This is particularly the case in a country like the UK, where we rank among the top 20 countries in terms of per capita GDP.

We see in other chapters the benefits and joys that are part of older age counteracting the more difficult aspects of life. Our exploration of the dark side indicates that even the darkest moments – fear of our own mortality, the loss of a loved one, the onset and development of dementia – offer opportunities for growth and reflection, helping us to get our priorities straight. These experiences allow us to value those who are dearest to us and what it is about life that we love and may help us to 'come to terms with death'.[23]

What needs to change?

We need to stop seeing old age as a time of dependency and deterioration, dementia and death. Instead we need to think in terms of a progression through the lifecourse where, at any stage, we may face difficulties and challenges.

At the same time we need to recognise that people are more likely to experience illness, death and bereavement when older than when young, and that our communities and society in general must recognise the need to offer support where needed and to ensure that older people are not excluded or side-lined just because they are near the end of their lives.

Death will come to all of us, and recognising this, talking about it and planning for it is also part of the lifecourse.

TWELVE

The best bits

Remember the Ian Dury song 'Reasons to be cheerful'? It informs us that there are constants in our lives – the best bits are to do with learning ('something nice to study'), friendship ('phoning up a buddy') and fun ('being rather silly').

Thirty-six years after this song was composed we updated the list by asking our interviewees to talk about their best bits. We structure this chapter around their lyrics:

- continuing to learn
- strengthening relationships
- gaining lots of freedom
- having fun.

The best bits need highlighting, as ageing is often associated with decline and misery and older age is perceived as dull and joyless – as we covered in the previous chapter. To combat negative images we need to see older people as 'assets rather than burdens ... active contributors, not passive recipients'.[1]

Continuing to learn

American psychologist Carl Rogers, still a practitioner at 78, talked about enjoying life: 'Increasingly I discover that being alive involves taking a chance, acting on less than certainty, engaging with life. All this brings change and for me the process of change is life. I realise that if I were stable and static it would be a living death.'[2] To learn, we need to be open to new ideas, feelings and risks.

We received similar messages from our interviewees. Learning brings pleasure and joy to older age. To illustrate these messages we draw on the success story of the U3A. Michael Young, who pioneered new thinking about active ageing in the 1980s, co-founded the U3A in defiance of 'chronologism' (judging an individual's capabilities solely by age). The U3A, entirely run by older volunteers, educates and stimulates people in their 'third age of life'. This was a brilliant idea, but its title is unfortunate. The 'third age', as we discussed earlier, is problematic, and so is the term 'university'. Barbara (68) explained to us that "it implies you have to be an academic, and that puts off working-class people". Nevertheless, the U3A offers valuable opportunities, as Barbara described:

> "People join because they want to learn. I like its philosophy. People lead groups voluntarily and therefore others don't pay for tuition. The self-help principle is crucial."

Barbara loves the U3A as she gets to know people in the community, makes friends and values being part of a growing network. She runs a philosophy group and goes to Pilates and badminton:

"We have good monthly meetings. Michael Rosen, who lives locally, showed a film he made on Hackney. Some people hold meetings in their houses, such as wheelchair users. They find that easier."

The U3A is growing in popularity and influence in the UK. In 2013 its membership rose to 900,000, with 570 centres and 13,500 different activity groups. It remains innovative, for example it helped to test MOOCs (Massive Open Online Courses) to look at ways of providing opportunities for in-depth study. In 2012 it provided speakers for a debate in the House of Lords, chaired by the Lord Speaker, Baroness D'Souza. The subject was: who should have responsibility for looking after the vulnerable in our society – the state, the family, or charities? U3A members discussed the issue alongside sixth-formers, reinforcing the importance of intergenerational learning and inclusivity.

A special effort is made to involve the over-80s, recognising that being engaged with others and connected to the wider society is crucial for their well-being, and the U3A places value on sharing their knowledge and expertise. Hackney's local newsletter states: "Without learning opportunities, residential homes can simply become places where society 'parks' the frail elderly while they await death. Residents can become over-medicated and under-stimulated." The idea that care homes can be learning hubs will challenge the ageist views of many, including policy makers.

Others get a huge sense of fulfilment from formal study. Online courses such as the Open University's make access relatively easy for older people. It's never too late to learn, as Gerald Nathanson's story demonstrates.[3] Gerald enrolled for evening classes when he was 74 and was awarded a BA in History from Birkbeck, University of London at 78. He grew up in war-time Britain and was evacuated twice as a child. By the time he left school, aged 15, he had been to 11 different schools. After the war he worked as a black cab driver for 42 years, and regretted not having had an education. He said:

> I soon realised that catching up on the education I had missed as a child wouldn't be easy … but I feel privileged to have experienced student life….
> The graduation ceremony was one of the proudest moments of my life.

Learning can be a huge challenge and source of pride. Mature students know that they can catch up. With support, learning is possible at any age. It is the values that older people hold – for example, aspiration and collaboration – rather than social class that are significant for learning, although financial resources and good health are important.

Gerald's success is inspiring but not exceptional. There are many similar stories. One Facebook message forwarded to us read: 'Scooter gran gets degree from Kingston University'. This headline is supposed to grab attention. 'Student in her 70s' doesn't have the same edge, although it is more accurate. There are countless courses available, many offered without qualifications. Some are designed specifically to consider the ageing process, such as two we attended called 'Growing into Ageing' and 'Older and Bolder', run at the City Lit in London.

In our researches we read about Annette (82), who found the course 'One Year to Live: facing issues relevant to end of life' important to managing her feelings and preparing for death.[4] The example of Annette, rejecting the view that older people have no more to learn and become dependent on others, shows how older people are empowered through learning and are able to face tasks and decisions that include the practical, medical, psychological, spiritual, legal or existential.

Older people are also meeting the challenges of new technology and enjoying new freedom. Ivy Bean gained more than 50,000 followers on Twitter before her death at 104, smashing the prejudiced view that old people are technophobes.[5] Older users are driving the growth in social networking, according to Ofcom, Britain's communications regulator. Daniel Thomas reported that technology is changing lives – helping people to live longer, more healthily and happily.[6] Janet (85) verified this important position when talking with us.

> "There are all sorts of things I want to do, mostly intellectual. I will continue to keep my brain active. This is seriously important. Age UK have technical classes and encourage people to take the opportunities to learn computer skills. I did a course with people who were learning computer skills – not for employment, they wanted to be part of the new world."

New technology is used by thousands of older people to promote autonomy and independence, reduce isolation, have fun and connect with online commerce, entertainment and communication.[7] Age UK recognises the importance of the internet in bringing people together as a community. Jude (70), who volunteers at an Age UK centre, told us that "older people really gain from the social contact in learning new skills in a group and feeling part of a neighbourhood community. They feel safe and supported."

Learning and creativity

The opportunity to find pleasure and a sense of fulfilment through creativity was reported to us with great enthusiasm. Tilda (89) talked to us about performing her verses: "I like being asked for a recitation. I like composing and performing. If I'd grown up in a different world I might have been a performer." Others mentioned continuing to write and share their love of writing. Margaret (70) spoke with pride: "I hope to finish writing some graded children's stories which I began when working abroad, and to write more sketches for our drama workshops."

Another success story shows that creativity can blossom much later in life. Toyo Shibata started writing at 92. Her poems are finding a huge audience in Japan. Her anthology *Kujikenaide* (*Don't lose heart*) has sold 1.5 million copies since its publication in 2009. She started writing after back pain forced her to give up classical Japanese dancing. In one poem, 'Secret', she writes: 'Although 98, I've fallen in love. I also have dreams. I want to ride on a cloud.' Bernadette (66) in her interview with us also talked of the fun that different forms of creative expression bring: "I want to have lots of fun, laughs, silliness and singing. That works wonders for me." Singing or playing instruments has been shown to have value in bringing all-round improvements to older people's lives. Participants in the national 'Music for Life' project led by Susan Hallam reported social, cognitive, emotional and health benefits.[8]

Learning and developing new identities

Many older people have a positive view of the next years of their lives and understand that they can take different paths into older age. For example, when physical problems limit one area of expression older people can reinvent themselves, as in Toyo's case. Liberation and joy can be found in creating new identities. This is complex learning. It may be a slow process, occurring over years as people think about themselves differently when freed from previous roles.

Toyo's case is an example of the way that previous identities can be cast off and new ones created. This is a process of active construction, suggests Anthony Giddens.[9] During the construction of identities we integrate new events into our accounts of our lives and make sense of them in terms of our life story. As Annie (66) told us, "I no longer tell people I am a head teacher. I tell them I am a writer." The life story, as in Annie's case, *is* one's identity, a continual process of making and remaking within the lifecourse.[10] The death in 2016 of David Bowie reminds us that a person can change, or create new identities, many times during a lifetime.

It is a liberating idea that people are the authors of their own changing identities and narratives and that we are able to create new, positive ways of being. And Annie observes that there is another dimension to be aware of – that other people may attribute particular identities to us: "People round here just see me just as a grandparent." This illustrates that our social settings are important in the formation of identity, and it is often hard to shake off limiting identities given by others, especially about being 'old' and how we should look and behave.

There may be losses and gains over a lifetime that may influence a person's way of seeing themselves. Diana Athill wrote:

> About halfway through my seventies I stopped thinking about myself as a sexual being, and after a short period of shock at the fact, found it very restful. To be able to like, even to love, a man without wanting to go to bed with him turned out to be a new sort of freedom. This realization was extraordinary. It was like coming out onto a high plateau, into clear, fresh air, far above the antlike bustle going on down below me. It was like becoming another sort of creature. Well, I

had in fact become another sort of creature: I had become an old woman! And to my surprise I don't regret it.[11]

Strengthening relationships

People talked with us, appreciatively, about having more time with their families and how, consequently, their relationships with partners, children and parents were thriving. Our survival as humans depends on social interaction, found most often within the family and close friendships. According to our interviewees, giving and receiving more attention, time, care and intimacy provides pleasure and delight.

Annie (66) is a case in point. She moved from London, once she had stopped working full time, to live in the same village as her daughter:

> "I didn't expect to live in Devon, close to my daughter, to spend my declining years. I like this intergenerational model, raising two grandsons. I love that. That's a surprise to me to be so family oriented."

Annie told us about a reciprocal relationship she had worked out with her daughter, who is still employed full time: "I want to spend more time with her but I am aware that she is busy. After work she wants to collapse. So I suggested that I made lunch once a week to take to her. I get to spend time with her and she gets a nice meal."

Ralph (82) pointed to the rewards in sharing life experiences with children and grandchildren, and Margaret (71) pointed out particular benefits: "Mixing more closely with families provides more stability for them and therefore for society." Grandparents provide £3.9 billion worth of childcare a year, as we describe in Chapter Four, on the economics of ageing, and rarely receive financial benefits in return for their time, even if they have given up paid work to take on the role.

There are more great-grandparents than ever before, as demographic change is affecting the make-up of families: family trees are now thinner, with fewer children in each generation but more generations alive together. One newspaper story revealed that around 10% of young children in Western societies have one great-grandparent.[12] The great-grandparent is such a recent anthropological phenomenon that its role is ill-defined and requires new learning. When Iris (69) spoke with us, she said:

> "My grandchild had a baby and expected me to look after her, as her mother works full time too. I picked up Daisy every morning and took her to my own home till six. That was OK till her cousin had a baby and expected me to do the same. I can't keep on doing it. I have my husband to look after who needs lots of care. I had to say 'No' and that took some doing."

In our interviews some people revealed that they do not wish to fulfil an active grandparenting role as is usually assumed will be the case. Some went as far as to say that they see such roles as exploitative. One said she had to "confess" to not wanting the role, suggesting this was perhaps a sinful attitude.

At least 20% of the UK population is child free, sometimes through choice. As most societies place a high value on having children and grandchildren, people who remain child free intentionally, or otherwise, are sometimes stereotyped as being selfish, avoiding social responsibility and being less prepared to commit to helping others.[13] However, increased freedom may allow time to engage in learning, creativity and political action. All of which benefit society. Diana Athill wrote:

> Now I have reached great-grandmother age, I dearly love certain young people of my acquaintance and am happy to have them in my life, but am I sorry that they are not my descendants? No, I much prefer thinking of them as surprising and very gratifying friends.[14]

Elizabeth (89) was grateful to her family. She told us: "I have a very attentive family, especially important now as all my friends have died off." One of the sad aspects of growing old is the loss of loved ones and close family members. But we report that many older people continue to find new relationships.

There was talk of love. "To love and be loved" is Bernadette's (66) recipe for a fulfilling life, and Margaret (71) was still hopeful of finding romance. She ended her interview by adding: "A final piece of whimsy – I am still looking for a nice man to take me punting on the river in Oxford – on a lovely summer's day of course. Failing that a cruise along the Panama Canal would do."

The idea of marriage or civil partnership is still compelling, regardless of age, report Euan Stretch and Ben Cusak.[15] Their account describes George Kirby, aged 103, getting married to Doreen Luckie, aged 91, in June 2015. They started 'courting' in 1988, when they met through an organisation that finds friends for mature people, and set up home together in 1990. Lesbian and gay couples are celebrating too. From March 2008 to 2012 there were 1,997 civil partnerships among the over-65s.[16]

For those finding love there is good news. A report by Relate says that relationships in later life promote good physical and mental health and protect against illness.[17]

While older people talk openly about love, their sex life is a taboo subject. Ruth (64) liked the opportunity to talk about sex to younger people before she retired from her role in a sexual health clinic:

> "I got a real buzz from confronting young people as an older person who knew about sex and was happy talking about it with them. When I told one of the young men who I'd got to know over the years that I was retiring, he was surprised and said that I 'Still had it going on'! I'm glad that there have been several films recently that show older people being sexual. Each generation thinks they invented sex, and in fact it was ours!"

Breaking this sexual taboo is important. Pamela Stephenson Connolly wrote:

> I have spoken to many octogenarians who enjoy frequent sensual contact and erotic fun (either alone or with a partner). They are not going to announce it to their families because, just like teenagers, they become acutely aware of ageist prejudices. It is time to lighten up about elder sex. Granny and grandpa are sexual beings. Get over it.[18]

Sexual ageism, like so many other prejudices, pervades our society. Older people's pleasure in sex needs to be celebrated, not denied.

The delights of living alone

In the UK 3.5 million people over 65 live alone. That is 36% of all people aged over 65.[19] The most common prejudice is that living alone is a miserable existence. However, the majority of those we spoke with highlight the joys of living alone. Tilda (89) said she hadn't expected to find it so interesting and rewarding: "I find it delightful living alone. I like making my own timetable." She spoke of her decision not to remarry:

> "I had one friend but it was not romantic enough to plunge into another marriage. I might not have married at all if things had been more permissive. The idea of another domestic 'knocking knees on either side of the fireplace' would have been going back to something I had for a number of years. I was brought flowers, and taken out but no physical aspect was wanted. It was a good friendship. We went on holidays abroad and to cottages and had seven or eight years of that."

Ruth (64) is quite comfortable being by herself and not feeling lonely when at home alone. She did, however, convey one possible downside:

> "Being out among groups of people, or after being out and about with friends and then coming home alone to an empty flat are times I experience loneliness. So there's an element of safety staying at home. Not going out could become unhealthy, but I'm a social person so I don't think that will happen."

Many older people value living alone, but others are lonely. We cover this issue elsewhere, as we do not wish to create the impression that everything in older life is wonderful. It certainly is not. We have complemented 'The best bits' with 'The dark side'.

Gaining lots of freedom and having fun

The sense of freedom that people gain as they get older was eagerly addressed by interviewees and often linked with decision making. The choices people make about what they do in later life are influenced, and sometimes restricted, by a sense of freedom.

The freedom to spend time as you wish and not having to work or get up for work can be wonderful. It is often reported how much older people enjoy life when work and social demands have been removed.[20] That 'free' time affords opportunities to be with family and friends, take part in interests and activities, to be creative, to travel. "I find it hard to imagine how I ever worked full time – that seems like another life," said Lorna (59). "Time is a huge benefit – when you have worked for 40 years you can do things you really love." Elizabeth (89) likes the idea that you can be very idle and let other people do all the work. William (82) likes more time for himself, time to read the paper and go to classes, whereas Janet (85) appreciates the joined-up nature of older age: "I enjoy life. I'm not chopped up in little bits. It's a continuum."

Social researchers provide evidence that women enjoy autonomy and pleasure in older age. Feminist scholar Bernice Neugarten reported this in the 1960s.[21] She found that older women rated their quality of life as high, in part because they relished the freedom offered as they escaped the constraints of traditional female roles. Fifty years after this finding, Amelia (64) talked to us about being carefree, especially after her children had left home, freeing her from the parental role, with positive effects:

> "The surprise has been the rediscovery of fun. I was a serious parent. I had not anticipated the rediscovery of freedom. We can go on holiday

at any time. I love that we say 'Shall we go to the cinema tonight?' and we can. We haven't got the kids criticising us. I am not the Mum, the responsible adult. I do feel sometimes the joyousness of youth, the irresponsibility."

Freedom is often symbolised by the concessionary bus pass. Those who had been using it for some time were really enjoying the advantages. The wider social benefits of this provision mean that fewer people are lonely, as they are able to travel free of charge. Amelia pleaded:

"Do not take away the bus pass! Many old people are depressed because they are isolated. We have to find some way to keep them involved and part of the community. Bus passes are critical. While waiting, they mingle with others at the bus stop and get out for a couple of hours. They are in charge of what they are doing. Without the bus pass lots of them could not afford that."

Evidence confirms Amelia's view. Of those eligible on the grounds of age in the UK, 77% own a bus pass and 52% use it at least once a week. Older people between 70 and 84, and more women than men, are significantly more likely to use the bus pass.[22] The social benefits are huge for this age group, and for women in particular. The senior rail card was also appreciated, allowing a third off travel costs.

A cautionary note was sounded by Ruth (64), however, who said that we need to think about older people who survive on just their state pension: "I think old age might only be fun if you're not struggling with money and are in the loop about free and cheaper activities."

Some ambivalence

While freedom to travel was key, Miriam (69) highlighted that this freedom has a downside "in comparison with the structures of work which take away a lot of the decision making that freedom brings". Don (72) confirmed that stopping work has many advantages, but he had been anxious at losing the structure of work. He was pleased that he had overcome the problem:

> "I can manage my own time instead of trying to fit my personal life into the worn-out corners of the day my employer left me with. Other people might not welcome the end of their routine as an employee and the structure it provides. I was nervous about that, but have found no problem at all filling my days."

For people who have been working for 40 years, freedom can be scary and adjustment takes time. Lisa (69) talked about the need to get her life in order before she could enjoy her newly found freedom:

> "It is nice to have some non-work time, though much of the free time now is spent in a prolonged phase of getting my life in order so I will have more free time! This organising phase is a surprise, though I could consider it a result of 'deferred maintenance' as I tended to other 'essential' duties previously."

Lisa's freedom is restricted by the need to tidy her life – that is now her main purpose. Research conducted by Susanna Ruskin reports that, over a certain age, people lack purpose.[23] One of her interviewees, Baroness Sally Greengross, said:

'For a lot of people this age (over 74) is when you can relax, but the danger is feeling that there's not much more to do'. Amelia (64) told us she was ambivalent. "I feel I should channel my energy into something worthwhile. Indulging myself and travel don't seem quite enough."

Enjoying being older

Most of our interviewees are enjoying life and are amazed by this. In answer to our question: 'What are the surprises in becoming older?' one frequent response was the enjoyment. Jack (72) remarked:

> "I did not think I would enjoy it so much. I was surprised how much easier life is when you are not working. I was surprised at never being bored. There are so many opportunities to do different things. The ageing process has slowed down for us – our generation. I expected to feel much older than I do at 72. Now I think that 72 feels like 52.… I don't find any problem in seeing my body getting older. I continually wonder that I can continue to play 18 holes of golf."

Miriam (69) was also surprised at still feeling young and "normal" and not what she had been fearing: "Being older has not been the unhappy experience that I anticipated, at least not so far." Others were surprised at feeling relaxed, as Lilian (70) explained: "It's lovely. I don't care what people think about me, so what if I have got varicose veins? If you don't like it don't look."

Jack (72) commented on the comfort of not having to do certain things any more:

"Because my energy level is lower I am happy not to dash up mountains. Lots of things that were important, like strenuous holidays and going to parties, aren't important any more. Been there, done that. It takes out things that worried you when you were younger. It is quite comforting."

We wonder why people are so surprised at enjoying life as they age. It seems that we are heavily influenced by the dominant message in our society of a miserable older life or, as Lorna Warren and Amanda Clarke so eloquently put it, 'the ubiquitous images of later-life as a worn-out, used-up decline into dependency'.[24] This image is not borne out by our research, as Jack implied:

"I don't have a problem about getting older. I don't regret anything.... I count my blessings that I don't have life-threatening illnesses yet. I can do all the things I want to do."

Jack, at 72, is approaching 'the perfect age', suggests Susanna Ruskin, who writes: 'According to a study based on data from The British Household Panel Survey, happiness declines from teens until the 40s, then picks up again until it peaks at around 74.' The secret of contented old age, according to her 74-year-old respondents, was:

- having a purpose and jobs to do;
- making everyday feel special;
- keeping busy to avoid darker moods; and in particular,
- having more time to spend with family.[25]

It's no secret. These principles are at the heart of a good and satisfactory life. Samantha (58) told us that "getting older is after all just another part of life which brings with it new challenges and exciting things … it is all about how you approach it".

Those aged between 65 and 79 tend to report the highest average levels of personal well-being, a recent ONS study found, but well-being ratings fall among the oldest age groups. Those aged 90 and over, however, reported higher life satisfaction and happiness as compared with people in their middle years.[26]

These surveys are important, as understanding how different age groups rate their personal well-being will help policy makers to target groups in most need and concentrate on issues that are fundamental to a good life. For example, the ONS study identified the potential need for interventions for those aged over 90, in how they feel that the things they do in life are worthwhile. This is especially important as we are now living longer, and one in three of babies born now will live to 100.

The stories we have collected about the 'best bits' show us that life in older age can be joyous. However, Lorna Warren and Amanda Clarke write that in attempting to counterbalance the ubiquitous images of decline it is important not to create new, unachievable oppressions of physically fit, creative, active, adventurous ageing.[27] We recognise the temptation to overdo the positive aspects that give weight to the active ageing rhetoric. While 'active ageing' is the strongest image in relation to what's good about ageing, this model is not appropriate for everybody and may represent a new tyranny, as we suggest in Chapter Three.

What needs to change?

Our society must not be trapped by images of older people defined by their disabilities, not abilities, but needs to take note of what people are now defining as a better ageing life.

The narratives presented here challenge negative perceptions, demonstrating that age does not diminish older people.

But, in order for more people to enjoy more 'best bits', we need:

- more examples of people achieving great things, to counteract stereotypes of 'scooter gran' for example;
- additional support facilities in the community that are freely available for all, such as those provided by Age UK;
- extra opportunities for people to continue learning wherever they live, including in care or nursing facilities;
- better, more frequent and more regular public transport, especially in rural communities;
- further subsidies for older people for tuition in colleges and universities;
- wider opportunities for befriending across the world, available through the internet.

We are certain of one thing: that learning, the strengthening of personal relationships, freedom and fun remain important at all stages of the lifecourse.

THIRTEEN

Wiser together

"Imagine the impact a ground swell of wisdom could have on empowerment and the development of skills and leadership in rural Africa and beyond." Maureen Groch described her vision and practice to Eileen, one of the authors, in October 2015. Maureen, known affectionately as Mo, moved from Johannesburg to rural South Africa eight years ago after she retired from 30 years in education. She said, "they needed a mentor, guide, facilitator, teacher and all-round grounded woman to build a school at the centre of the village". Mo has met many wonderful people of similar mature years who have expressed the desire to find a way they too could contribute to improving social and human conditions. Some have even expressed envy. "For me the way forward is clear", said Mo, "to tap into the global wisdom of so many who have reached retirement. There is immeasurable wisdom which could have a huge impact on so many in the world today."

Rather than defining old age by an increasing inability to do things, as in the deficit model, older people need to be recognised for their wisdom and their skills in supporting others and in helping to bring about change in communities and in society. To ignore older people's experience and wisdom is senseless and heartless – a further example of ageism, suggesting that older people have nothing to offer. We are not surprised that some expressed envy when they saw what Mo was doing in South Africa. She is using her skills, talents and wisdom to bring about important changes in a remote community and she is thriving. Other people, who do not have such opportunities, expressed their frustration to us. For example, Ray (74), who had been a surgeon, said, "It's such a waste. I could be a mentor or use my wisdom in other ways in an advisory capacity. I have so many transferable skills and it's as if nothing I did in my professional life has any value any more. I feel I am on the scrap heap."

We do not take an idealised view that age confers wisdom or that wisdom derives from age – indeed, research suggests that wisdom does not depend on age;[1] but we do examine the potential for experience to add to knowledge, create learning and lead to actions that can benefit both communities and society, as in Mo's case. There is benefit from individual wisdom and wanting to use it to good intent, and there is potential benefit to the whole community.

Answers to our research question on the benefits of ageing took us by surprise. Many people had at the top of their list: "acquiring wisdom, and having a more reflective outlook"; "becoming wiser, humbler and more stoic"; "being seen as valuable holders of living history"; and "producing creative wisdom". As wisdom, and the potential to do great things, was so frequently mentioned by our interviewees we felt this single theme deserved separate analysis.

Here we consider:

- the benefits of individual wisdom;
- wisdom – a social and interactive phenomenon;
- drawing on and sharing older people's wisdom for the benefit of the whole community;
- applying wisdom within an age-inclusive society.

The benefits of individual wisdom

Throughout history older people in communities – sages, chiefs, statesmen and women, gossips, priestesses and priests, and teachers and mentors like Mo – are named and renowned as having particular skills, qualities, levels of expertise and wisdom. In the United States the term 'Elders' is used in this way, as in the Eldering Institute we describe later, and it is echoed in the archaic 'Alderman' of English councils. Older people are valuable resources. Not only do they share their own insights, but they help others to be wise. In his examination of the long tradition of wisdom in *The Greek Way of Life*, professor of classics Robert Garland talks about 'true wisdom' being seen as the function of old age.[2] The idea of wisdom as a function of older age may be fading, but our researches illustrate that this is far from the case.

Older people, usually men, have often been recognised as valuable resources in society. In a treatise called *Should the Elderly Run the Country?*, the Greek scholar Plutarch made a strong case in favour: 'Whereas young men bring the gifts of their bodies to the State, the old bring the gifts of the soul, the psyche, which Plutarch lists as justice, moderation and wisdom.... Athens reserved different roles for women past childbearing age, such as midwifery and mourning.'[3] Plutarch's treatise might be more correctly entitled *Should Elderly Men Run the Country?*, given the sharp differentiation of gender roles that sadly still exists in many societies. For example, we have referred earlier to the way that older women are portrayed today in our culture, and rarely employed in the media.

The qualities of wise individuals

'Perspicacity' and 'sagacity' are splendid words describing components of wisdom, drawn from Robert Sternberg and

Elena Grigorenko's research.[4] Other components include the expeditious use of information, reasoning ability, learning from ideas and environment, and judgement. In her research Ricca Edmondson identifies features that have been ascribed to wise people, including being at home with oneself, being insightful, being content, being calm in the face of crisis and having an eye for what's important.[5]

In our own research, interviewees talked about developing wisdom through experience and reflection, resulting in a clear perspective to act with confidence and make sound decisions. These observations accord with findings from other research in the field. For example, Gary Kenyon suggests that wisdom is the ability to exercise good judgement about important and uncertain matters of life, such as new problems, or for which there are competing or conflicting solutions.[6]

Older people are better able to live with contradictions in life, Kenyon suggests, as they see the essentials of situations from their greater experiences. When we observe the age of most leaders of countries, heads of state or governments, we can see that this point has resonance. It was noteworthy, for example, that Barack Obama was only 47 when he became the US president, the youngest person ever to assume the role.

Several of our interviewees were still in paid employment. They talked about how wisdom was acknowledged in the workplace in how people acted in particular situations, especially around pacing themselves, coping with problems and speaking with authority. Veronica (58) said other people "dash around, take no time for themselves and then they burn out and are not fit for anything, whereas I can still keep going". Amelia (64) added that big problems didn't seem quite as overwhelming. Other views suggested that surviving difficult periods makes people stronger; emotional strength follows a process of reflection; good leadership brings authority.

This culmination of emotional strength and authority in shaping one's outlook was expressed in what Jane (70) had to say. She talked about "less angst":

> "by that I mean not getting so worried about things because I have experienced them before. I get a feeling of superiority from having solutions and not having to re-invent the wheel in all sorts of situations. I have increasing confidence and am less in awe of authority. I can face new challenges....
> I am prepared to 'have a go' at things I might not have had a go at earlier. I don't mind making a fool of myself."

From our researches we understand that individual wisdom:

- is the ability to think and act judiciously, drawing on knowledge, experience and insight;
- involves an understanding of people, events and situations;
- requires prudent emotional reactions;
- needs good judgement as to what actions should be taken, and a realisation of what is of value in life, for oneself and others.

These attributes are important and when placed within social situations can be transformatory.

Wisdom: a social and interactive phenomenon

Seeing wisdom as a 'quality of life rather than a commodity' and 'a matter of being rather than having' allows us to view it as something that can be learned.[7] Wisdom is within the reach of everyone, rather than the sole province of experts, educators or therapists. Accordingly, everyone has access to 'ordinary wisdom'. This is not acquired automatically. It requires reflection and learning.

In line with this view, wisdom can be created through people's interactions 'rather than from the insights of one outstanding individual'.[8]

The social aspect of wisdom is rarely discussed, and older people's potential to apply their wisdom to issues about ageing and the age-inclusive society are frequently overlooked. For example, Tom (62) thought that his experience helped him to maintain relationships. "I am now far more sensible. I think more now about how the way I talk might affect other people. It is certainly helpful and it takes the volatility out of relationship decisions."

This example illustrates that the function of wisdom is more usefully seen as an interactive phenomenon.[9] Some of our interviewees remarked that their growing self-assuredness and wisdom gave them courage to make decisions about intervening in social situations. Maureen (80) said:

> "I do things on the spur of the moment, for the sheer hell of it. For example, giving chocolate to make peace in a warring family I passed in the bus shelter."

This capacity to 'defuse situations of conflict with wit, humour and charm' and treat people with affection and respect is important in social wisdom.[10]

Flora (58) told us that she had wisdom to share with younger people in her family. Lorna (59) voiced a similar view, saying that she would like to shape younger people's experience of what "old looks like" as a liberated and wise person:

> "I'm very aware in extended family terms, especially with the younger generations in Ireland

and England, of being a link to the past. I no longer have many friends who are older than me so socially so I've become 'the old ground breaker', which can be frightening, and makes me feel even older, but I try to give a positive take on ageing and model it to younger friends and family as liberation more than decline."

These accounts of making peace in a warring family, sharing experience with younger relatives, and helping to shape younger people's experience of what 'old looks like' all demonstrate the 'intent to do good' – an attribute that Kenyon identified as central to wisdom. This good intent depends on holding favourable attitudes toward other people and its deliberate use to improve others' well-being.[11]

Other socially focused attributes gleaned from Ricca Edmondson include: being engaged with others and being curious, feeling free from a superficial need for other's approval and having independence of mind. Wise people acting in social situations demonstrate kindness, are humble, brave and have courage, as illustrated by Maureen's story.

Creating wisdom through dialogue

One of the most effective ways that wisdom can be learned is through dialogue. In our interviews we uncovered two examples of wisdom generated in this way. Annie (66) said:

"I am extraordinarily lucky to do this – ageing – in the company of others. I belong to an interesting intellectual community, exciting, good talking about it, lights coming on, new thinking, that's always good."

Dialogue is not conversation. Dialogue focuses on the possibilities for learning, sometimes described as 'interthinking', a reciprocal process in which ideas are bounced back and forth to create learning.[12] It is carried out with reflection and analysis to construct knowledge by piecing ideas together to gain new insights on what might change.

The second example came from Bernadette (66):

> "I love talking with friends at a sustained level about the issues of becoming older. It transforms how I think. We get to an understanding that I couldn't reach alone. It's exciting, feels creative and affects my perceptions of being older, my outlook and behaviour."

Wisdom through dialogue comes about through the creation of new ways of thinking and acting, quite difficult to do alone, as it requires:

- questioning, finding patterns and explanations, connecting and adding to previous knowledge;
- recognising that there are things not known;
- appreciating the value of doubt and ambiguity; and
- freeing people to see their own behaviour in a new light.

We three authors belong to a Retiring Women group that has been meeting for over 10 years. We like to think that this is an example of an intellectual community where wisdom is generated. Creating an intellectual community where wisdom is generated isn't just an intellectual process of reflection and learning. It is about offering emotional support, and security to allow others to think, see, feel or act in new ways.

The strength of this group is that it can provide validation – supporting people in making changes. It challenges and extends our learning, as belonging to a network rich in support, trust and information provides resources that help our understanding and new ways of seeing and acting.

Men-only groups exist but are fewer in number. One such group, in which all the participants were senior managers taking early retirement, took part in a research project.[13] The men found the transition challenging and needed regular support and dialogue over several years.

These examples illustrate that social wisdom isn't the gift of wisdom from (usually) the old to others – it is not a commodity. Rather, social wisdom is produced with others, through dialogic processes. These are important at all our levels – in groups, in the community, as well as in society.

Identifying principles for wisdom in action

On a related theme the Eldering Institute came up with principles for 'wisdom in action'.[14]

1. Responsibility: owning our circumstances and choosing how to respond. Not placing blame or taking credit for our lives or the world as it is but responding in unprecedented ways.
2. Completion: appreciating and letting go of the past to be present in conversations. Not allowing the past to limit and determine choices and actions.
3. Respect and compassion: being patient and trusting, acknowledging that everyone learns at their own pace and can transform their circumstances.
4. Authentic communication: listening non-judgementally to each person's perspective, experience and ideas.

5.   Humility: acknowledging our limitations and humanity.
     Working with others in collaborative ways, rather than
     persuading or manipulating them.
6.   Service: caring and connecting to other people, creating
     new possibilities for others. Contributing and valuing the
     best of who we are.

These principles suggest ways in which groups, communities
and societies could act with wisdom. Many groups of
older people and groups of people of cross-generational
composition include such principles. They may be implicit,
however. Making them explicit by considering the values on
which practice is based is likely to encourage wise practices.
Ricca Edmondson speaks of 'wise societies' in her book
Ageing, insight and wisdom, suggesting that it is something to be
aimed at, both by individuals and by societies: wise societies
might be expected to contain and support wise individuals.[15]

How refreshing it would be to see these principles
enacted in the way in which politicians, policy makers and
broadcasters speak with each other, rather than in arguments
based on competition, posturing and point scoring.

Drawing on and sharing older people's wisdom for the benefit of the whole community

Older people have a significant role in their families and in
their communities in using and sharing their wisdom. Here
we discuss the ways in which their wisdom is put to good
use. We examine the advice that older people give about
ageing, how they hold and share memories, unite different
generations and support community action.

Advice about ageing

Wise people are often asked for their advice about getting older, as they are known to make good judgements, are knowledgeable, sincere and act consistently with their ethical opinions.[16] In researching for our book we wanted to hear about the advice our interviewees would give to others about ageing.

In a typically wise response, Ruth (66) said: "I don't think I can give advice to other people. We're all so different and have such different experiences." Ruth is acknowledging that the giving of advice may be counter to the role of enabling others to learn and reach decisions for themselves. However, when pressed, she said:

> "I guess the only thing is perhaps being open to new people, experiences and ideas. It's too easy just to close down and await the inevitable. Though I forget this advice when I'm feeling low!"

Several people commented on the necessity of shifting perceptions of ageing from its being a long slow decline to being a process of affirmation: "Make the best of everything – find lots of 'bests' to relish", suggests Elizabeth (89), while Flora (58) warns against both covering up signs of ageing and acting old: "Embrace the good things and don't get hung up on preventing age happening, like having cosmetic surgery. Don't see ageing as something negative and at 60 don't start wearing beige."

The second area of advice focused on valuing and nurturing relationships, seen as crucial for a joyous older age. Hannah (54), Lisa (68), Margaret (71) and Pauline (74) made these observations:

- it is even more important to keep in touch with friends;
- maintain and expand friendships as people you know may move away or die;
- have friends of all ages and find new ones with different spheres of interest;
- keep up with family and loved ones – use telephone, texting and Skyping.

Bernadette's (66) advice was to forgive people for anything they have done to offend and not to bear grudges. She suggested reviewing one's relationships: "Don't go on seeing people if friendships aren't working any more. It's a waste of time and their influence may limit your outlook."

Keeping on learning, and remaining interested and interesting, was other advice offered. This included being adventurous and, again, not acting old. Lilian (70) said: "Don't restrict yourself to things old people do. Go to Glastonbury, learn a new language, instrument, skill. Use your knowledge and wisdom – campaign, mentor a child, work on a support phone-line." Others drew attention to the importance of developing interests before retiring. Jack (72) said he would have hated to learn new skills from scratch, adding, "If you already have interests they will flourish."

Holding and sharing memories

Societies have long relied on oral traditions to preserve records, as Lorna (59) reminded us: "older people are valuable holders of living history and creative wisdom". In previous generations elders in a community held memories – society's encyclopaedias. In the internet age, Jared Diamond suggests that older people's memories have shifted in their importance to the function of holding family histories.[17] Maureen (80) agreed:

"I'm conscious now that I'm holding the history of my family and I want to collect it all for the next generation. I have wanted to do this since a very old friend died and I noticed that her children didn't know some things about her."

This process of handing down and preserving memories for future generations is a way that older people's knowledge is mediated into wisdom. It is a realisation about what is important for future generations – knowing about the family's place in history. Formal reflections become a dynamic process as younger people examine the information and make sense of their own lives. Miriam (69) told us about her research into her ancestry that demonstrates this potential for learning.

Learning about family and forebears: a case study

When Miriam retired she became interested in knowing more about her ancestors. By the time she became interested, both parents had died. She was an only child, as was her mother, while her father was the youngest by 15 years in his family, so there was really no one she could ask for first-hand information. She realised then that if she did not record what she knew, her children and grandchildren would have even less idea about their ancestors.

"It had started to matter to me as I wondered about personalities, traits, occupations, physical appearance and health of my ancestors and how those things might have impacted on the person I am. I felt that I needed to know more about the contexts I was born into, and this would be a way of measuring how I had done in life. If I felt like that maybe my children and grandchildren would too. I have no religion and believe that there is no afterlife. If this life is all that there is, remembering people and passing on some knowledge of them prolongs their impact on the world and makes their lives more meaningful."

Miriam started, as others usually do, by constructing a family tree. But just drawing up a map did not appeal:

"What I found most interesting was personal details, more than the bare facts of births, deaths and marriages. I have written an account of my own life, that of my parents and as much as I know of my grandparents and their families, including photographs. Even this limited account goes back well into the 19th century and gives some idea of family origins and roots.

"There is some satisfaction in having recorded as much as I can from my own knowledge of my family. I have no one with whom I can share experiences of childhood, but I have loving children and grandchildren who may one day be interested to know more about their ancestors. One of my grandsons who is now five is always asking about 'the olden days' and seems genuinely interested to know how things were different."

This is a beautiful gift from a wise parent to her children and grandchildren.

Sharing memories more widely

Oral projects frequently draw on the memories of older people to bring history to life. For example, during 1998 and 1999, 40 BBC local radio stations recorded personal oral histories from a broad cross-section of the population for the series *The Century Speaks*. It drew on the feelings, attitudes and ways of life of older people, to create vivid pictures of the past.

Older people's stories enliven museum collections that otherwise can be inaccessible for children. Older people's visits to history classes can be more engaging than reading history textbooks. And children's visits to older people's residential homes and community centres can result in valuable learning experiences too. Older people can be witty and entertaining teachers, and have a wealth of experience to share. And most importantly, these occasions unite generations, as we observe in such programmes as *The Listening Project* on BBC Radio 4, based in the British Library. In this programme, people share an intimate conversation with a close friend or relative that helps to build a picture of life today.

The history of local communities, and of countries, also needs to be accessed through the memories of older people as well as documents and artefacts.

Uniting different generations

Older people have a central place within families and help to make life good. Neighbourhoods and communities are made better too, more united and inclusive places. There are countless stories of kindness, generosity and support provided. Lilian (70), remembering her own experiences as a child, is inspired to offer what she can:

> "I think enabling people to live as full a life as possible is important – being part of the community and having a role. I look after a friend's small daughter regularly. It helps her, but much more important I enjoy it, and want to be part

of a family network. And, you don't have to be hugely fit either. I remember when I was a child an elderly, wheelchair-bound neighbour taught me to knit. It was a real sanctuary for me. I came from a big family and needed her attention."

This intergenerational reciprocity provides important connecting and bonding experiences. We collected many examples of people wanting to be kind and supportive in small ways, as Samantha (58) said to us:

"Tell people if they look nice, tell them how you feel about them. Buy them that bunch of flowers to say thanks. If they think you're a bit bonkers let them, best to tell them, than wish that you had and it be too late."

While these may seem to be small acts, their effects may be huge.

Kindness is really appreciated by older people, as Elizabeth (89) explained. "I appreciate being taken out in the wheelchair. People are very kind, the ones you know and the ones you don't. I value that."

Ruth (64) pointed to the importance of having friends across a wide range of ages, and remaining in cross-generational communities. "Having younger friends reinforces my desire to live in the community as long as possible, instead of moving to sheltered housing. I want to live among a mix of ages, even if that means putting up with noisy neighbours." Living with younger people helps people to stay youthful, as Mary (83) told us. She fosters two boys aged 11 and 14. We draw on her story in Chapter Fourteen.

So, as well as contributing millions to the UK economy in both elder and childcare and volunteering, older people can give their kindness and generosity to others. In doing so they unite families and communities, providing essential social glue.

Tapping into global wisdom

Two projects provide further examples of the power of older people's sharing of their wisdom. These highlight education for empowerment and radical change.

Mo, whom we introduced earlier, set up a school in the Londolozi village in the Sabi Sand Reserve in South Africa. Mo saw the project as a holistic process offering education and support to single mothers, orphans, people who have lost loved ones to HIV/AIDS, survivors of violence or those who are malnourished. The focus of the programme is on digital access to information, English language skills, personal and leadership development, skills for future employment involving creativity, collaboration, critical thinking and problem solving. Mo explained:

> "People's problems cannot be separated from education, as emotional issues can inhibit learning. We have to uphold value systems and help individuals find hope and purpose, empower girls and students to support their peers. And we have to learn from each other.… in this space not everyone has a grandmother, a mother or even a sibling. We need to balance education and life skills. We're extremely passionate about that."

Most of her days now are spent in the surrounding villages working under the banner of the Good Work Foundation.[18] Her experience has profoundly influenced her thinking. "Although daunting", she said, "it has been a time of great learning. I have learned far more than I have taught." Mo believes that education is the catalyst that can change society:

"Education must be underpinned by a human-centred philosophy and should facilitate the growth of learners, of all ages, to become the best possible versions of themselves. Investment in individuals will spread into communities and the sphere of influence grows.… I can't say there was no fear in the decision. I was leaving behind everything I knew to move to the bush. But often such change brings a new energy that allows us to grow.

"What I like about the model is its 'Africanness'. Ubuntu is an African word that has community as its centre and that is what we are creating. Education must be available to our preschool children and grandparents. The door is open for community members to approach us and other members of the community welcome them. We have built a space based on trust and meaningful relationships. Parents and children are graduating together. That's quite something, isn't it?"

Mo is often asked "How can I change my life in a meaningful way?", indicating how many older people are looking to do good acts. Many individuals she has met go on to support the Foundation. She would like to inspire more retired people, not only teachers, who ask how they can contribute. She concludes: "Education needs leaders with passion and wisdom. Who wants to retire anyway – there are far better things to do. I feel privileged to have a significant role in solving one of the challenges facing humanity."

A second project, 'Skype Grannies', has a similar philosophy. Volunteers use Skype to help some of the world's poorest children to teach themselves. These volunteers, who may not be grandparents, help people very far away from their own communities. For example, at the 'school in the cloud'

Lorraine Schneiter, a former Open University tutor, calls a group of children in India. And then they chat. Lorraine is one of hundreds who talk to, read with and encourage schoolchildren. This project is the brainchild of Sugata Mitra, a 64-year-old professor of educational technology at the University of Newcastle.[19]

Applying wisdom within an age-inclusive society

Older people have the capacity to play a crucial role in society through sharing their wisdom, especially when formal work ends. They inspire, unite families and communities. Societies need to recognise this potential and have systems and structures in place to utilise older people's wisdom.

Sadly, a number of older people whom we interviewed said their wisdom was a wasted resource. Margaret (71) said, "we have no meaningful input into society any more. Our slowly gained wisdom is not required." Elizabeth (89) confirmed this ageist predicament:

> "They don't listen to my opinions, because I am old. I don't offer them. I know about things…. Wisdom is not that well received. It's one of the reasons why care for the elderly is such a mess – because older people's views are not heard."

Margaret's and Elizabeth's wise observations need to be heard, in a process of dialogue, to inform intergenerational thinking and action, alongside thousands of others. It is a disgrace that this is not happening, reflecting the ageist views that older people have nothing to offer. We need to support the creation of communities and societies in which older people's wisdom can flourish and is used to inform decisions. Yvonne Roberts suggests that:

It is imperative that older people are involved in the design and delivery of services and support not just for their own age group but also for the community ... we need to recognise that ageing has reached a new frontier that requires different tools to carve out a better future.[20]

Other groups and organisations should follow Age UK's lead in championing the voices of older people on national and regional levels, and include older people in consultative and research groups.

What needs to change?

Older people must not remain untapped resources in our society. Opportunities to create wisdom, to mentor, give counsel, volunteer, guide, facilitate and teach should be the norm, not the exception. Wisdom needs to shared, created and applied through social practices, in community decision making, for example. These practices need to be facilitated so that cross-generational dialogue can be effective and bring about change.

As social wisdom does not lie within individuals, but results from interaction between people, wisdom can become embedded in the ways that age-inclusive communities and societies make decisions, such as in informing best practices in living together (see Chapter Nine) and in the ways that communities look after older people (see Chapter Ten).

Principles and practices need to be established to develop age-inclusive groups and communities so that there are opportunities to share wisdom. Regardless of age, people need to be:

- included in decision about their lives;
- involved in democratic practices about the community they live in;
- asked to identify their needs and appropriate levels of support;
- respected, valued and treated with affection;
- engaged in dialogue to come up with creative solutions to the issues of an ageing society – to avoid repeating the same old patterns.

In age-inclusive dialogue, concepts such as decline and dependency are rejected and artificial divisions – between the young and old, and between healthy and unhealthy – are removed.

In a wise, age-inclusive society we need to ask of every decision that is made and every policy enacted: is this in the best interests of everyone, and is it a deliberate action to improve the well-being of all?

FOURTEEN

We're still here

'From the beginning of time there have been two flames burning in the human heart. The flame against injustice, and the flame of hope that you can build a better world. And my job is to go round fanning both flames.' This is how Tony Benn summed up his career in politics.[1] His words and actions remain an inspiration.

Political activism for our generation growing up in the 1950s and 1960s began by lobbying government to introduce or stop legislation, for example, around abortion and women's right to choose, setting up self-help groups and refuges, taking direct action, either on a large or small scale, such as living at Greenham Common or canvassing for a Labour candidate in the February 1974 general election. We were vociferous at political meetings, on women's committees and in trade unions, marching and leafleting for CND (the Campaign for Nuclear Disarmament) and Anti-Apartheid. As Lynne Segal suggests, 'entering old age, almost all those leftists and feminists I knew forty years ago hold much the same political views now as then. There is no shortage of older radicals who continue to support struggles for justice, equality and a safer, greener, more peaceful world.'[2]

In our researches we came across many people who are still active in local, national or international politics and are still vociferous in campaigning for a better world in many ways and in fighting ageism. Annie (66) told us:

> "This generation is not going to accept being treated like fools. There are more of us for a start, our attitudes are different, more of us are better educated, we are more critical, less deferential and know things can change. Sexist and racist jokes horrify us now so there will come a time, soon, when everyone will find ageist jokes abhorrent."

In this final chapter we

- apply our learning from feminist politics in combatting ageism;
- consider how political commitments sustain people into older age; and
- examine the ways in which older people remain socially and politically active, believing they can still make a difference in shaping the culture of their era.

The end of the chapter is a celebration of older people through stories of their social and political activity, demonstrating that we continue to be subversive while retaining power, dignity and courage.

Feminism and ageism: what can we learn?

The feminist movement brought about change by challenging all aspects of sexist behaviour at individual, societal and political levels. We learned the dangers of separating groups of people, of powerful hierarchies and exclusionary practices.

We were very active in that movement and now we apply our learning about change in combating ageism. Writing this book is part of that ambition, especially to express older people's sense of injustice and to identify what needs to change.

We remain hopeful. Bernadette's (66) story reminds us that important changes do happen:

> "I remember trying to get a hire-purchase agreement for a washing machine in the early 1970s and the sales assistant saying I would need my husband's signature. I told her I was a lesbian and she said well in that case you will have to wash your clothes by hand. At that time we fought for equal rights for women and we were successful to a degree, but never imagined a time when we would have gay and lesbian civil partnerships and same-sex marriage too. Now it's the time for older people to be seen positively."

As Anne Karpf suggests, 'We may come to view both ageing and the denial of age as enduring but now discredited historical relics.'[3]

Just as feminists did, we want the age-integrationists to define, establish and achieve equal political, economic, cultural, personal and social rights for older people. We believe that the movement should be inclusive. For example, feminist advocacy mainly focused on women's rights until some feminists, including bell hooks, argued for the inclusion of men's liberation because men are also harmed by traditional gender roles.[4] We believe that the age-integration movement should include young people, as they too are harmed by the separation of 'young' and 'old' and pressure, for example, to cover signs of ageing. We call on younger people's participation in stamping out ageism, as we see it as an important strategy for achieving full societal commitment to age equality and achieving the larger goals of equality across all divisions. We celebrate the work being done in schools. For example, Maria (45), a primary school teacher, told us about her work in personal, social and health education lessons with her Year 3 class on the uses and abuses of cosmetics, and is discussing what ageing means in philosophy classes. The Fabulous Fashionistas, the older women who made their name in the now famous television programme, visit secondary schools to challenge the barriers between young and old by presenting positive images.

We also need to acknowledge the existence of completely different ways of looking at older people in different cultures, such as in the East and in the Southern Mediterranean, where they are venerated and valued for their wisdom and experience. This is not the model we are emulating, but we can learn from it.

And throughout the book we have referred to the valuable work of the New Dynamics of Ageing Research projects, and also the work of Age UK in challenging ageism.

Political commitment in the lives of older people: the fight continues

'Never doubt', Margaret Mead once said, 'that a small group of thoughtful, committed citizens can change the world. Indeed, it is the only thing that ever has.' This view, which informs our vision, is echoed in Steve Crawshaw and John Jackson's book *Small Acts of Resistance*, reminding us that the history of the past hundred years bears witness to the fact that the individual conscience, ignited by indignation, is capable of almost anything.[5]

But older people are not generally considered to be radical – a view brought about from the perspective of disengagement theory. This stereotypical view is far from the truth. In our researches we have come across many examples of older people who are still fighting for political causes. As Barbara (68) told us, political activity is a still major part of her life:

> "I still want to make a difference and contribute to the positive aspects of my community and the wider world. I take part in Board meetings for management of NGOs [non-governmental organisations] and schools and I gain social contact with like-minded people and a sense of purpose.
>
> "I would add that the danger can be of taking on too many voluntary roles and not giving space for oneself and taking advantage of being retired, such as reading, gardening walking and visiting friends. All the things that are so important but easily sacrificed."

Political activity sustains many older people, giving them purpose and social benefits, as Barbara explained, and sometimes the older people get, the more radical they become. The late bishop of Stepney, Trevor Huddleston, who had dedicated his life to the Anti-Apartheid campaign in South Africa, told Molly Andrews: 'I've become more revolutionary every year I've lived. And certainly now, because life is so much shorter.'[6]

In her book *Lifetimes of commitments*, Molly Andrews reports on the enduring significance of political commitment throughout the course of a lifetime. She looked at the life histories of 15 men and women interviewees aged between 70 and 90 who had worked for progressive change for a half-century or more. Most were ordinary men and women who, 'despite, or perhaps because of, their advanced years', remained committed to securing social justice when called upon for support. Each explained that, just as it always had been, it was politics that still gave meaning to their lives.

Eileen Daffern (late 70s) said: 'It gives you a motive for going on living. It's very strong. It is survival.'[7] Others in their 80s were just as confident that socialism was a goal worth fighting for.

The underlying message in Andrews' book is that some people sustain their radical outlook throughout their lives and their fighting spirit sustains them. The interviewees were certain that one day, however distant, their goals would be met.

This sentiment is reinforced by Anne Karpf, who states that while ageing inevitably brings losses and usually some physical deterioration, those who remain engaged with life manage to maintain a positive ratio of enthusiasm to resignation: 'The ones who fare best not only care what they leave behind for the next generation, but are also able to keep learning from people both older and younger than themselves.'[8]

It is clear from these accounts that many older people will not collude in a social conspiracy that makes them invisible, passive and silent.

We also want to report how organisations are fighting ageism and shaping social policy. We take one example.

The Older Women's Commission

Labour MP Fiona Mactaggart set up the Older Women's Commission, and a number of TUC women officials are members. At a meeting we attended in 2014 the subject debated concerned discrimination and the culture of bullying older staff at top and middle management levels. Older women workers are often given the worst shift patterns, as if to move them towards the door – one example of the difficulties that older workers face. Su Patel, a retail worker, Union of Shop, Distributive and Allied Workers representative and member of the TUC Women's Committee, told us that she was on her feet for eight hours at a time, without a break for five hours and not allowed a chair or stool. She experienced abuse and had to work unsocial hours. Lack of sufficient notice of shift changes made her life difficult, as she was caring for a sick relative. She was disciplined for being away because of the shift changes imposed, and received written warnings. These are not unusual issues. Some older workers have to work long hours, as they need extra money to support their children and grandchildren. When they are not at work they may be caring for older relatives.

Ageism functions because the majority of workers (persons who are not old) are treated as the norm and are the more valued group. Older people, 'the others', are treated as lesser beings – for example, getting the worst shifts – and may be less visible – for example, working in the storeroom rather than in the shop. They are treated as second-class citizens and hidden from view. This includes older women in the media, particularly in television, a point discussed earlier.

Important steps are being taken jointly by the Commission and the TUC around the introduction of 'adjustment leave' when spouses or other family members are ill. Steps are also being taken for attitudes to older workers to change. 'Look at what am I doing (working, contributing, being as capable and efficient as younger people) not what I look like' is one of their slogans – reframing the issues to focus on values. The TUC is working towards stronger employment laws, informing the training of managers, changing the culture of the workplace, influencing the content of management training courses and serious enforcement of employment laws, as well as public campaigning to create a different sort of climate. The need for older women, who would understand the issues, to be in the boardroom is crucial. At the same meeting we attended in 2014, Kay Carberry, the Assistant General Secretary of the TUC, said: 'Change in attitudes will come from change in practice.'

No shortage of older radicals

Political and social action is undertaken by millions of older people and we have countless stories of their work as trustees, mentors and coaches, magistrates, school governors and in volunteering overseas. Anne Karpf points out that older people's reduced energy seems more than compensated for by the increased amount of time they have. 'One reason that old people give for volunteering is personal growth – yes, even at 90 ageing like this doesn't seem quite so bad.'[9]

Older people are fighting for justice and fairness, are providing love and support for their families and are supporting communities and global issues. Joseph (68) told us:

> "By a convoluted route I have ended up not as a champion of the proletariat, but as a fighter for the rights of small farmers worldwide. Which is of course fitting, because all my ancestors were peasant farmers, and I now wear the badge with pride, and I've got the T-shirt. True!"

To counter the negative messages about older people we present some of their stories. These come from people who are subversive and strong and have great wisdom, dignity and courage. These narratives show a range of different activity and at many levels – in their homes, in their communities and globally. This is a fitting end to the book, as it demonstrates the value of older people in the world and how the world couldn't do without them.

These examples include:

- individual action to combat ageism and to challenge the image of decline and disengagement;
- action for the community;

- supporting families, the community and society; and
- global action.

Individual action to combat ageism

Many professional people are challenging ageism in different ways. As an 82-year-old actor, Dudley Sutton is confronting audiences with the intimate routine of an older man's daily life in *Have Your Circumstances Changed?*. The project features three 'elderly' men and three young boys whose interactions invert the relationship between adult and child. The question is: 'Is the boy the man's past or his future, or someone who will grow up and make political decisions about elder care?' Sutton is interested in the way society both ignores and patronises older people and sees radical, thought-provoking theatre as an excellent medium to fight ageism.[10]

In another field of the arts Caroline, one of the authors, is using her writing skills to blog for the visibility of older women. She strongly believes that we need to see images, read books, watch plays and films about those who are less visible in our world than the white, middle-aged, male or young person. 'We are still here! Our voices still count', she proclaims:

> In 2011 I set up my blog called *Bookword*. It's about all things bookish. Periodically I review fiction about older women. I began to do this after a course I attended about growing older only had examples from literature related to men: Odysseus, King Lear, Prospero. Where, I wondered, were the older women? So I began with *Mrs Palfrey at the Claremont* by Elizabeth Taylor, which explores some of the painful and amusing aspects of being older and not cared for by your family. I have reviewed sixteen novels since then. There is a

list of about 50 novels on the blog that include strong older women. It turns out that there are plenty of bold, feisty and resolute older women in fiction; some hate the idea of dying, some live as they always have, some take on new challenges, some are brilliant and some are ill or suffer from dementia. In each review I say something about the character of the older woman and what I value about it. You can add to it if you like.[11]

Challenging the image of decline and disengagement

Mary, now 83, is fostering two teenage boys – resisting her grown-up children's suggestion to downsize. What nonsense – she needs the space to continue to look after young people who need support, care, love, kindness and a stable home environment. Mary and her husband, John, were astonished when they received an MBE in the 2013 New Year's Honours List in recognition of being good citizens for their lifetime's work as foster parents. Mary said she laughed all day when she heard the news. She is a very modest woman who has helped many tens of young people to lead happy and secure lives.

Action for and in the community

Martin (72) told us about his work as chair of a local development trust. He thought that as the council has limitations on what it can do we must ask what we can do for the community.

> "I began as the Chair of the Trust and introduced three or four new people. We work with Community Gardens, and the Gardening for Health scheme, which takes referrals from GPs as well as local people who turn up and about 15

school children from The Grove primary school. This has now amalgamated to form the Totnes Trust – an umbrella organisation for community projects – and this has connected me to ATMOS, of which I am a director." [ATMOS is an ambitious town project to reuse the old Dairy Crest site by the railway station for community use.]

By making the older people visible in the community and giving them a platform, another project nudged people into rethinking their attitudes. Annie (66) described to us how action by 'The Grandmothers' project had the effect of challenging attitudes towards older women. This community arts project by Devon-based Encounters Arts brought together 14 grandmothers over five months in 2015. They met to share themes such as loss and gain, youth and age, fight and defeat and what it is to be a grandmother and an older woman today – many of the themes we have explored in this book. Annie said:

"The project culminated in three performances. The audience feedback demonstrates how people were challenged in a quiet way. The highlight, according to one person was 'to see elderly women speak at last'. Another said, 'it was really great to hear women who are older given a platform to be seen and heard'. Another said it achieved 'an opening up of a subject which is too often ignored. It touched and stirred me.' Another, 'it grew my respect for grandmothers'. And another said she or he realised 'that I love my Nan and can't wait to speak to her'."

This is an example of a community project that enabled learning about ageing for individuals and for their community.

When it comes to pressure groups, energy and experience is such an asset, reports Moira Petty.[12] Across the country, she writes, local groups are reviving local facilities, plugging gaps in services not supplied by commercial companies and protecting the natural landscape. And almost without exception, it's older generations spearheading this grassroots action. Here are three examples.

Debbie Cosgrove (58) leads the appeal to buy Blencathra as a community asset. Her group successfully fought off five rival buyers and hopes soon to announce ownership of the mountain, part of the Lake District National Park, to protect its future.[13] Debbie sees it as an opportunity to engender social responsibility and to encourage disadvantaged youth, those with health problems and physical and learning disabilities, to enjoy Blencathra.

Barry Forde (66) leads a £3 million self-help project to bring one of the world's fastest broadband connections to rural communities. By the end of 2015, Broadband for the Rural North will have connected 5,000 properties in 35 outlying parishes. Local people, ranging in age from 50 to 90, have done everything from funding the project to digging trenches, laying cables and providing a 'help service' for users. Barry said: "I often think it is not so much the broadband as the community spirit that people really enjoy."

Martin Booth (62) helped to organise a meeting of 350 locals to refurbish the Hudswell village pub in the Yorkshire Dales that closed in 2008. A year later the group set up a community cooperative, issued shares and was awarded a community enterprise grant. The new pub includes a shop that the village hadn't had for 30 years, a lending library, free internet access and allotments. The book club meets every month and the shop is open seven days a week, run by volunteers. Martin said: "It's drawn everyone closer and newcomers are absorbed more easily into the village. It's been so rewarding. I look at the people chatting in the pub and shop, and it makes me smile."

Supporting families, the community and society

We note in so many stories that older people are generous and want to help others as much as they can. Take Mike's story, for example. When Mike was 70, in 2014, he started training for the triathlon and raised £7,000 for the charity War Child. Mike was himself a war child, born three months after his father was killed in the battle for Caen in 1944. As he was so successful he was asked by the charity to support other fundraisers with their campaigns. Mike also acts as a full-time carer to support his wife, Nina, who has Parkinson's disease. He told us that the triathlon will help keep him in good shape for her. He completed the triathlon again in 2015, raising another £3,500. He has also set up a new community choir so that residents can get involved socially and have fun.

Antoinette (72) explained to us how she supports the mothers of young people who are in prison. She told us that her son was arrested and spent a few weeks in jail and during that time she befriended younger women who were raising their families single-handedly and on little money. Even though her son is now out of prison she continues to help other women with all the bureaucracy, translations, meetings with solicitors and accompanying them to see their children in prison, which is often a harrowing experience.

Jean (88) is an actress, and during periods when she has no employment she works as a Samaritan. She told us that not only does she support people on the telephone and visitors to the centre on a long shift every week but she trains new Samaritans on courses and supports new recruits in a mentoring capacity.

Global action

An individual older person's values often motivate their ambitions. For example, Anne (72) reported to us, after being involved as a Games Maker in the 2012 Olympics, that she has turned her attention to the Iranian and Kurdish Women's Rights organisation, developing a pack of materials for schools to recognise violence and other abusive practices toward girls and women. She is also spearheading a project with universities in less-affluent countries to develop in-country doctoral programmes. This will enhance the skills and experiences of university staff and allow students to work and to stay with their families while they study for their higher degrees. The project takes her to Kenya, Pakistan and other destinations.

What we can take from these stories

These examples demonstrate how the lives of many older people are selfless, value driven, modest, imaginative, supportive, kind, generous, inventive, wise, sensitive, intelligent, loving and compassionate.

We applaud organisations and projects, like all the ones mentioned here, that do not exclude older people acting as volunteers.

We take inspiration from the belief that 'There has never been a better time to age ... to challenge the narratives of decline and age resistance, and seek out other people in the growing age-acceptance movement'.[14] To rephrase Hillary Clinton's famous declaration about women's rights: Human rights are older people's rights and older people's rights are human rights, once and for all!

What needs to change?

There is still a lot to do to fight ageism, in providing a more nuanced framing of people as they age, particularly in relation to their being seen as active politically and contributing to the welfare of their families, communities and globally. At every stage of life people need to be recognised as wanting to learn, meet challenges, achieve astonishing acts and contribute to society.

Policy makers and community leaders must recognise that many older people remain socially and politically active and can still make a difference in shaping political views and policies. Their voices need to be heard when decisions are made. This is a politically active generation and needs to be recognised as such. There must be no age bar set against people contributing to society, and employment laws need to be seriously enforced. Older people must not be hidden in back cupboards. We all need to confront the social conspiracy that makes older people invisible, passive and silent.

The examples of the contributions of this generation must stop being seen as exceptional. It's not just middle-class, rich people who want to have a say. People from across the social spectrum continue the political fight.

FIFTEEN

Our vision for the future

Increased life expectancy affects everyone, individually, in families and in communities, as well as society as a whole. We have already entered the new age of ageing.

Here is our vision for the future.

The challenges of the demographic changes are met on all levels. All decisions are made in the best interests of older people, as much as of the rest of the population. Demographic change is not seen as a problem but as timely and comprehensive. To cater for the continuing challenges of the new age of ageing, planning is undertaken by individuals, families, communities and policy.

Older people are not treated as 'others' but are part of an inclusive society. Prejudice and discrimination against older people are seen as human rights and social justice issues. Basic economic provision is assured. Older people are integrated within the workplace and community and into social activities in ways that encourage them to share their knowledge, experience and learning. Everyone is treated in this way.

Young people understand that they will get old and do not fear age or see it as a separate phase of the lifecourse. The culture has changed so that those who want to do so are encouraged and supported to make use of the freedom that later life has brought them and to seek adventure and continued learning. Older age is seen as a time of joy.

If we three thoughtful, committed citizens can visualise this future, then the vision can be one step towards changing our society. We believe that if we can describe this vision, then it can be achieved.

Together let's challenge:

- the view of old age as deterioration and dependence and the idea that life in old age is less attractive than an early death;
- the laws and policies that are made without thought for older people;
- political and social debate that blames older people for society's problems;
- discrimination against and segregation of older people in accommodation, the media, the marketplace, at work, everywhere.

Together let's take action and:

- scrutinise all policy decisions to ensure that they are in the best interests of older people as much as those of any others;
- promote different ways of thinking and talking about older people that will enrich our understanding of older age;
- address the inequalities, unexplored assumptions, prejudices and derision of older people and recognise beauty in older age;
- provide respectful care, appropriate to the individual;
- demand full integration of health and social care;
- campaign for state provision of everyone's basic needs – warmth, food, accommodation and transport;
- insist on sufficient funds for research into age-related diseases;

- create forums and other opportunities for older people to share wisdom, learning, achievements and generosity, and to contribute to society.

These actions towards the vision will make life better for all of us, not just for older people. And they will ensure that people who are young now will live better, and in a fairer society, when they reach older age.

Notes

Chapter One

[1] Pharaoh, G. (2015) 'My Last Word – July 2015', www.yesiambovvered.com (accessed 28 September 2015).

[2] ILC-UK (2016) *Tomorrow's world: The future of ageing in the UK, planning tomorrow today*, London: ILC-UK.

[3] ONS (2016) *At what age is personal well-being the highest?* London: Office for National Statistics.

Chapter Two

[1] De Gray, A. (2004) 'We will be able to live to 1,000', BBC News, http://news.bbc.co.uk/1/hi/uk/4003063.stm (accessed 10 August 2015).

[2] Delphi234 Wikimedia.org/wiki/File%3AUKpop2010.svg (accessed 29 February 2016).

[3] ONS (2015a) *Ageing of the UK population*, www.ons.gov.uk/peoplepopulationandcommunity birthsdeathsandmarriages/deaths/bulletins/childhoodinfantandperinatal mortalityinenglandandwales/2015-03-10 (accessed 10 August 2015).

[4] ONS (2015b) *Life expectancy at birth and at age 65 by local areas in England and Wales 2012 to 2014*, www.ons.gov.uk/peoplepopulationandcommunity/birthsdeathsandmarriages/lifeexpectancies/bulletins/lifeexpectancyatbirthandatage65bylocalareasinenglandandwales/2015-11-04 (accessed 29 January 2016).

[5] ONS (2015b).

[6] Beach, B. and Bamford, S-M. (2014) *Isolation: The emerging crisis for older men*, London: ILC-UK.

[7] ONS (2015c) *Childhood, infant and perinatal mortality in England and Wales, 2013*, www.ons.gov.uk/peoplepopulationandcommunity birthsdeathsandmarriages/deaths/bulletins/childhoodinfantandperinatal mortalityinenglandand wales/2015-03-10

[8] Blastland, M. (2012) 'Go figure, when was the real baby boom?', BBC News, 2 February (accessed 21 October 2015).

[9] ONS (2013a) *Women in the labour market*, www.ons.gov.uk/ons/dcp171776_328352.pdf (accessed 21 October 2015).

[10] ONS (2013b) 'Around one fifth of women are childless at age 45', www.ons.gov.uk/ons/rel/fertility-analysis/cohort-fertility--england-and-wales/2012/sty-cohort-fertility.html (accessed 21 October 2015).

[11] Cangiano, A. (2014) 'The impact of migration on population growth', Migration Observatory Briefing, COMPAS, University of Oxford (February).

[12] Eurostat (2015) *Eurostat statistics explained: Population structure and ageing*, http://ec.europa.eu/eurostat/statistics-explained/index.php/Population_structure_and_ageing (accessed 11 August 2015).

[13] WHO (2015) *World Health Statistics 2015.*

[14] Seager, J. (2009) *Penguin atlas women of the world*, 4th edn, New York: Penguin.

[15] OECD (2014) *Life expectancy at birth*, www.oecd.org/els/family/CO1_2_Life_expectancy_at_birth_1May2014.pdf (accessed 11 August 2015).

[16] Newcastle University (2015) Diabetes Research Group, www.ncl.ac.uk/medicalsciences/research/groups/diabetes.htm (accessed 11 August 2015).

[17] Boseley, S. (2015) 'Dementia not the epidemic it was feared to be, say academics', *Guardian*, 21 August.

Chapter Three

[1] 'Vieillir au Quebec – l'agisme ordinaire', www.ledevoir.com/2004/03/08/49235.html (accessed 3 September 2015).

[2] Edmondson, R. and von Kondratowitz, H.J. (2009) 'Establishing a humanistic gerontology – challenges and opportunities', in R. Edmondson and H.J. von Kondratowitz (eds) *Valuing older people: A humanist approach to ageing*, Bristol: Policy Press, p 2.

[3] Butler, R. (1975) *Why survive? Being old in America*, New York: Harper and Row, p 12.

[4] Carlson, M. (2010) 'The life of Robert Butler', *Guardian*, 18 July.

[5] Calasanti. T. (2008) 'A feminist confronts ageism', *Journal of Aging Studies*, vol 22, no 2, pp 152–7.

[6] Phillips, J., Ajrouch, K. and Hillcoat-Nalletamby, S. (2010) *Key concepts in social gerontology*, London: Sage.

[7] Bytheway, B. (2011) *Unmasking age: The significance of age for social research*, Bristol: Policy Press.

[8] Coupland, N., Coupland, J. and Giles, H. (1991) *Language, society and the elderly: Discourse, identity, and ageing*, Oxford: Blackwell.

[9] Atchley, R.C. (1999) *Continuity and adaptation in aging: Creating positive experiences*, Maryland: Johns Hopkins University Press.

[10] Karpf, A. (2014) *How to age. The school of life*, Basingstoke: Pan Macmillan, p 42.

[11] Weisman, A. (1882) *Über die Dauer des Lebens*, Jena, Germany: Verlag von Gustav Fisher. Cited in Gavrilov, L. and Gavrilova, N. (2002) 'Evolutionary theories of aging and longevity', *The Scientific World Journal* vol 2, pp 339–56.

[12] Gavrilov, L. and Gavrilova, N. (2006) 'Reliability theory of aging and longevity', in E.J. Masoro and S.N. Austad (eds) *Handbook of the biology of aging*, 6th edn, San Diego, CA: Academic Press, pp 3–42.

[13] *Little Britain* is a BBC television programme.

[14] Gullette, M.M. (2004) *Aged by culture*, Chicago: University of Chicago Press.

[15] Havighurst, R.J. (1961) 'Successful aging', *The Gerontologist*, vol 1, pp 8–13.

[16] Austin, C.D. (1991) 'Aging well: what are the odds?' *Generations*, vol 15, no 1, pp 73–5.

[17] Guarente, L. and Kenyon, C. (2000) 'Genetic pathways that regulate ageing in model organisms', *Nature*, no 408, pp 255–62. Cited in Gavrilov, L. and Gavrilova, N. (2002) 'Evolutionary theories of aging and longevity', *The Scientific World Journal*, vol 2, pp 339–56.

[18] Shoard, C. (2015) 'Jane Fonda: plastic surgery bought me 10 years', *Guardian* G2, 22 May, p 10.

[19] Erikson, E.K. (1997) *The life cycle completed*, New York: W.W. Norton.

[20] Athill, D. (2015) *Alive, alive oh!* London: Granta Books, p 158.

[21] Soden, S. (2012) 'Redefining cultural roles in older age: grandmothering as an extension of motherhood', in V. Ylanne

(ed) *Representing ageing: Images and identities*, Basingstoke: Palgrave Macmillan, p 98.

[22] Couvee, K. (2015) 'People call you dear and then treat you like an idiot', *Islington Tribune*, 5 June, p 3.

[23] Phillipson, C. (1982) *Capitalism and the construction of old age*, London: Macmillan.

[24] Willetts, D. (2010) *The pinch: How the baby boomers took their children's future – and why they should give it back*, London: Atlantic Books.

[25] Walker, A. (2012) 'The New Ageism', *Political Quarterly*, vol 83, no 4, pp 812–19.

[26] Giele, J.Z. and Edler, G.H. (eds) (1998) *Methods of life course research: Qualitative and quantitative approaches*, London: Sage Publications.

Chapter Four

[1] Ipsos Mori (2014) *Grandparents and their grandchildren*, poll on behalf of Grandparents Plus (11 July 2014), www.ipsos-mori/researchpublications (accessed 6 October 2015).

[2] Walker, A. (2012) 'The new ageism', *Political Quarterly*, vol 83, no 4, pp 812–19.

[3] Spijker, J. and MacInnes, J. (2013) 'Population ageing: the timebomb that isn't?', *British Medical Journal* (12 November).

[4] Bingham, J. (2013) 'Take less, bishop tells baby boomers', *Daily Telegraph*, 11 June, www.telegraph.news (accessed 12 June 2013).

[5] Lloyd, J. (2015) *Young against old? What's really causing wealth inequality*, London: TUC.

[6] Mullan, P, (2000) *The imaginary time bomb: Why an ageing population is not a social problem*. London: I.B. Tauris; Walker, A. (2012) 'The new ageism', *Political Quarterly*, vol 83, no 4, pp 812–19; Spijker, J. and MacInnes, J. (2013) 'Population ageing: the timebomb that isn't?', *British Medical Journal* (12 November).

[7] Walker, A. (2012) 'The new ageism', *Political Quarterly*, vol 83, no 4, pp 812–19.

[8] Walker, A. (2012).

[9] Willetts, D. (2010) *The pinch: How the baby boomers took their children's future – and why they should give it back*, London: Atlantic Books.

[10] Howker, E. and Malik, S. (2001) *Jilted generation: How Britain has bankrupt its youth*, London: Icon.

[11] Spijker, J. and MacInnes, J. (2013) 'Population ageing: the timebomb that isn't?' *British Medical Journal* (12 November).

[12] Piketty, T. (2014) *Capital in the twenty-first century*, trans. Arthur Goldhammer, Cambridge MA: The Belknap Press of Harvard University Press.

[13] Ipsos Mori (2014).

[14] Cox, A. (2011) *Age of opportunity: Older people, volunteering and the big society*, London: ResPublica.

[15] OECD (2016) *Statistics: Social expenditure tables*, https://stats.oecd.org/Index.aspx?DataSetCode=SOCX_AGG (accessed 1 February 2016).

Chapter Five

[1] Hatfield, S. (2014) 'Why is advertising not aimed at the over-50s?', *Guardian*, 3 December, www.guardian.co.uk (accessed 4 March 2015).

[2] Walsh, J. (2011) 'Old bats out of hell', *Independent*, 28 January.

[3] ActiveAge (2012) 'The ageing marketplace: how some companies are successfully addressing the needs of the older consumer, whilst others are struggling to access this expanding market', www.activeage.org, p 5 (accessed 7 October 2015).

[4] ActiveAge (2012).

[5] Sinclair, D. (2010) *The golden economy: The consumer marketplace in an ageing society*, London: ILC-UK for Age UK.

[6] Age UK (2015) Money matters factsheet: 15 May.

[7] ActiveAge (2012).

[8] Stroud, D. and Walker, K. (2013) *Marketing to the ageing consumer: The secrets of building an age-friendly business*, London: Palgrave Macmillan.

[9] Age UK and Brunel University (2012) *Ageing consumers: Lifestyle and preferences in the current marketplace*, Report of the Age UK Engage Business Network.

[10] Age UK and Brunel University (2012).

[11] Age UK and Brunel University (2012).

[12] Walsh, J. (2011).

[13] Stroud, D. and Walker, K. (2013).

[14] Cox, E., Henderson, G. and Baker, R. (2014) *Silver cities: Realising the potential of our growing older population*, IPPR North, www.ippr.org/publications/silver-cities-realising-the-potential-of-our-growing-older-population (accessed 17 August 2015).

[15] ActiveAge (2012).

[16] Jones, H. (2015) 'Beware pension fraudsters', *Choice*, May.

[17] Brignall, M. (2011) 'Setting off alarm bells', *Guardian Money*, 2 April.

[18] Hatfield, S. (2014) 'Why is advertising not aimed at the over-50s?' *Guardian*, 3 December, www.guardian.co.uk (accessed 4 March 2015).

[19] Blaikie, A. (1999) *Ageing and popular culture*, Cambridge: Cambridge University Press.

Chapter Six

[1] ONS (2015) *UK labour market*, London: Office for National Statistics.

[2] Cox, E., Henderson, G. and Baker, R. (2014) *Silver cities: Realising the potential of our growing older population*, IPPR North, www.ippr.org/publications/silver-cities-realising-the-potential-of-our-growing-older-population (accessed 17 August 2015).

[3] Sinclair, D. (2015) *The myth of the baby boomer*, London: Briefing for Ready for Ageing Alliance.

[4] PRIME (2015) *The missing millions: Illuminating the challenges of the unemployed over 50s*, London: BITC.

[5] Maitland, S. (2010) *Working better: The over 50s, the new work generation*, Manchester: Equality and Human Rights Commission.

[6] TUC and CIPD (2011) *Managing age*, new edn, London: Chartered Institute of Personnel and Development.

[7] Tinsley, M. (2012) *Too much to lose: Understanding and supporting Britain's older workers*, London: Policy Exchange.

[8] TUC and CIPD (2011).

[9] Yeomans, L. (2011) *An update of the literature on age and employment*, London: Health and Safety Executive, p xi.

[10] Maitland, S. (2010).

[11] TUC (2014) *Age immaterial: Women over 50 in the workplace. A TUC Report*, London: TUC.

[12] TUC and CIPD (2011).

[13] TUC and CIPD (2011).

[14] CIPD (2012) *Flexible working provision and uptake*, London: Chartered Institute of Personnel and Development.

[15] National Association of Pension Funds (2012) 'Over-50s set to live longer but not prosper', press release, 30 November (now Pensions and Lifetime Savings Association).

[16] PRIME (2015).

[17] Age UK (2010) *Agenda for later life 2010: Our five-year ambition for public policy*, London: Age UK.

[18] TUC (2014).

[19] PRIME (2015).

[20] Tinsley, M. (2012), p 6.

[21] Altmann, R. (2015) *A new vision for older workers: Retain, retrain, recruit*, Report to the government, March, London: Department of Work and Pensions.

[22] Tinsley, M. (2012).

[23] Age UK (2013) *Agenda for later life 2013: Improving later life in tough times*, London: Age UK.

[24] Sinclair, D. (2015).

[25] Age UK (2015) 'New bid to fight age discrimination in job markets', press release, June, www.ageuk.org.uk (accessed 6 June 2015).

Chapter Seven

[1] Frenkiel, O. (2015) 'Why I rejected gagging clause', *Guardian,* 8 January.

[2] Karpf, A. (2014) 'Embrace your years', *Guardian,* 4 January.

[3] Freedland, J. (2015) 'If Hillary Clinton wins, she will bury the "old woman" slur', *Guardian*, 3 January.

[4] Lessing, D. (1973) *The Summer before the Dark*, London: Jonathan Cape Ltd.

[5] Labour Party (2013) *The Commission on Older Women: Interim report,* London: Labour Party.

[6] Mills, E. (2014) 'Don't you dare call me granny', *Sunday Times*, 23 November.

[7] White, C., Morrell, G., Luke, C. and Young, P. with Bunker, D. (2012) *Serving all ages*, Creativity Diversity Network for the BBC.

[8] New York Film Academy (2015) *Gender inequality in film*, https://www.nyfa.edu/film-school-blog/gender-inequality-in-film/ (accessed 18 October 2015).

[9] Variety (2015) *Meryl Streep finances screenwriters lab for women over 40,* http://variety.com/2015/film/news/meryl-streep-women-screenwriters-lab-1201475337/ (accessed 18 October 2015).

[10] Freedland (2015).

[11] Mangan, L. (2014) 'Is it OK to lie about your age?', mangan@stylist.co.uk (accessed 10 January 2014).

[12] Featherstone, M. and Hepworth, M. (2005) 'Images of ageing: cultural representations of later life', in M. Johnson (ed) *The*

Cambridge handbook of age and ageing, Cambridge: Cambridge University Press.

[13] Warren, L. and Richards, N. (2012) 'I don't see many images of myself coming back at myself: representations of women and ageing', in V. Ylanne (ed) *Representing ageing: Images and identities*, Basingstoke: Palgrave Macmillan.

[14] Evaristo, B. (2013) *Mr Loverman*, London: Hamish Hamilton.

[15] Featherstone and Hepworth (2005).

Chapter Eight

[1] ABC News (2011) 'Pageant mom gives Botox to 8-year-old daughter: how young is too young?', 12 May, by Hagan, K., Kunin, S. and Ghebremmedhin, S. via *Good Morning America* (accessed 23 June 2015).

[2] *The Kyle Report*, ITV, 5 February.

[3] Holland, C. and Ward, R. (2012) 'On going grey', in V. Ylanne (ed) *Representing ageing: Images and identities*, Basingstoke: Palgrave Macmillan, p 129.

[4] Hopkins, K. (2015) 'Beauty is big business for Britain', *The Beauty Economy*, 27 September, p 1.

[5] Morrell, C.M. (2003) 'Empowerment and long-living women: return to the rejected body', *Journal of Aging Studies*, vol 17, pp 69–85.

[6] Featherstone, M. and Hepworth, M. (1991) 'The mask of ageing', in M. Featherstone, M. Hepworth and B.S. Turner (eds) *The body*, London: Sage.

[7] Gadow, S.A. (1986) 'Frailty and strength: the dialectic of aging', in T.R. Cole and S.A. Gadow (eds) *What does it mean to grow old? Reflections from the humanities*, Durham, NC: Duke University Press.

[8] Brooks, A. (2004) '"Under the knife and proud of it". An analysis of the normalization of cosmetic surgery', *Critical Sociology*, vol 30, no 2, pp 207–39.

[9] Kinnunen, T. (2010) '"A second youth": pursuing happiness and respectability through cosmetic surgery in Finland', *Sociology of Health and Illness*, vol 32, no 2, pp 258–71.

[10] Beausoleil, N. (1994) 'Make-up in everyday life: an inquiry into the practices of urban American women of diverse backgrounds', in N. Sault (ed) *Many mirrors: Body image and social relations*, New Brunswick, NJ: Rutgers University Press, pp 33–57, at p 51.

[11] Gimlin, D. (2000) 'Cosmetic surgery: beauty as commodity', *Qualitative Sociology*, vol 23, no 1, pp 77–98.

[12] Christie, B. (2015) *A book for her*, London: Century Books. Extract printed in *The Guardian*, 20 June 2015, G2, p 9.

[13] Bartky, S. (1990) *Femininity and dominance: Studies in the phenomenology of oppression*, New York and London: Routledge.

[14] Observer Woman Magazine (2009) 'The New Male Vanity', *Observer*, Sunday, 11 January 2009, p 33.

[15] Gilleard, C. (2005) 'Cultural approaches to the ageing body', in M.L. Johnson (ed) *The Cambridge handbook of age and ageing*, Cambridge: Cambridge University Press, p 160.

[16] Hopkins, K. (2015) 'Beauty is big business for Britain', *The Beauty Economy*, 27 September, p 1.

[17] Woolf, N. (1990) *The beauty myth*, London: Vintage.

[18] Bordo, S. (2003) *Unbearable weight: Feminism, western culture and the body*, Berkeley and Los Angeles: University of California Press.

[19] Coupland, J. (2007) 'Gendered Discourses on the "problem" of ageing: consumerized solutions', *Discourse and Communication*, vol 1, no 1, pp 37–61.

[20] Andrews, M. (1999) 'The seductiveness of agelessness', *Ageing and Society*, vol 19, no 3, pp 301–18.

[21] Featherstone, M. and Hepworth, M. (2005) 'Images of ageing: cultural representations of later life', in M.L. Johnson (ed) *The Cambridge handbook of age and ageing*, Cambridge: Cambridge University Press.

[22] Hughes, S. (2015) 'Life begins at 70', *Guardian Weekend Magazine*, p 25.

[23] Hughes, S. (2015), p 25.

[24] *Daily Mail*, 19 February 2015, p 1.

[25] New Dynamics of Ageing (2012) *Representing self-representing ageing. Look at me!* Images of Women and Ageing, www.newdynamics.group.shef.ac.uk/assets/files/NDA (accessed 24 June 2015).

[26] Martin, R. (2010) *Look at me! Images of women and ageing*, www.representing-ageing.com/workshops.php (accessed 24 June 2015).

[27] Warren, L. and Richards, N. (2012) 'I don't see many images of myself coming back at myself: representations of women and ageing', in Ylanne, V. (ed) *Representing ageing: Images and identities*, Basingstoke: Palgrave Macmillan, p 168.

[28] Karpf, A. (2014) *How to age*, London: Macmillan.

[29] Mailonline (2015) '"I wanted to have my own face": Jane Seymour, 63, and Jacqueline Bisset, 69, speak out against Botox and say they've aged naturally', 20 February, www.dailymail. co.uk/tvshowbiz/article-2568136/Jane-Seymour-63-Jacqueline-Bisset-69-speak-against-Botox-say-theyve-aged-naturally. html#ixzz3SHtLCSmq (accessed 24 June 2015).

[30] *The Graham Norton Show*, BBC television, 3 October 2014.

Chapter Nine

[1] Wood, C. (2013) *Top of the ladder*, London: DEMOS.

[2] Hussey, S. (2001) 'Rural Women 1918–50', in L. Botelho, and P. Thane, *Women and ageing in British society since 1500*, Harlow: Longman/Pearson.

[3] Gawande, A. (2014) *Being mortal: Illness, medicine and what matters in the end*, London: Wellcome Foundation, pp 66–8.

[4] ONS (2013a) *What does the 2011 Census tell us about older people?* London: ONS.

[5] UNESCO (2009) *Integration and participation of older persons in society*, Policy brief, On Ageing no 4, November.

[6] ONS (2016) *At what age is personal well-being the highest?* London: Office for National Statistics.

[7] Beach, B. (2015) *Village life: Independence, loneliness, and quality of life in retirement villages with extra care*, London: ILC-UK.

[8] Wood, C. (2013).

[9] The Elderly Accommodation Council, www.eac.org.uk.

[10] Sinclair, D. (2015) *The myth of the baby boomer*, London: Briefing for Ready for Ageing Alliance.

[11] ONS (2013a).

[12] Anderson, P. (2016) 'Young renters have it hard, but it's even worse if you're older', *Guardian*, 16 February.

[13] Griffith, M. (2011) *Hoarding of housing: The intergenerational crisis in the housing market*, London: Intergenerational Foundation.

[14] Malik, S. and Roberts, Y. (2011) 'Should over-60s be asked to move to smaller homes?', *Guardian*, 24 October.

[15] Wood, C. (2013).

[16] Piketty, T. (2014) *Capital in the twenty-first century*, trans. Arthur Goldhammer, Cambridge MA: The Belknap Press of Harvard University Press.

[17] ILC-UK (2016) *Tomorrow's world: The future of ageing in the UK, planning tomorrow today*, London: ILC-UK.

[18] Nazroo, J. (2005) *Ethnic inequalities in quality of life at older ages*, ESRC-funded Research L480254020, www.esrcsocietytoday. ac.uk (accessed 17 August 2015).

[19] ONS (2013b) *Measuring national well-being – older people's neighbourhoods, 2013*, London: ONS.

[20] Bamford, G. (2005) 'Cohousing for older people: housing innovation in the Netherlands and Denmark', *Australasian Journal on Ageing*, vol 24, no 1, pp 44–6.

[21] Addley, E. (2015) 'Old friends pioneer new model for retirement homes', *Guardian*, 16 February.

[22] Whateley, L. (2015) 'Grin and share it', *Guardian Weekend*, 13 June.

[23] Williams, Z. (2014) 'Retirement village where silver foxes bit back', *Guardian*, 25 January.

[24] Sherwood, H. (2014) 'Homes for the brave', *Guardian*, 22 November.

[25] Joseph Rowntree Housing Trust (2008) 'The Garden Village of New Earswick', leaflet, York: Joseph Rowntree Housing Trust.

[26] Cadywould, C. and O'Leary, D (2015) *Community builders*, London: DEMOS.

Chapter Ten

[1] Victor, C. (2015) 'Class, care and caring', in M. Formosa and P. Higgs (eds) *Social class in later life*, Bristol: Policy Press.

[2] Hofstede, G. (2001). *Culture's consequences: Comparing values, behaviors, institutions, and organizations across nations* (2nd edn), Thousand Oaks, CA: Sage Publications.

[3] Gawande, A. (2014) *Being mortal*, London: Profile Books Ltd.

[4] Carers UK (2015) *Caring into later life: The growing pressure on older carers*, London: Carers UK.

[5] Carers UK (2015).

[6] Carers UK (2015).

[7] Age UK (2015) 'Factsheet 10: Paying for permanent residential care', www.ageuk.org.uk/Documents/EN-GB/Factsheets/FS10_ Paying_for_permanent_residential_care_fcs.pdf?dtrk=true%5D (accessed 2 November 2015.)

[8] Breeze, E. and Stafford, M. (2008) 'Receipt and giving of help and care', in J. Banks, E. Breeze, C. Lessof and J. Nazroo (eds) *Living in the 21st century: Older people in England*, London: Institute for Fiscal Studies.

[9] NICE Guidelines (https://www.nice.org.uk/guidance/ng21) (accessed 21 May 2015.)

[10] ONS (2014) *Changes in the older resident care home population between 2001 and 2011*, London: ONS.

[11] Forder, J. and Fernandez, J.-L. (2011) *Length of stay in care homes*, Report commissioned by Bupa Care Services, PSSRU Discussion Paper 2769, Canterbury: PSSRU

[12] Geripal (2010), www.geripal.org/2010/08/length-of-stay-in-nursing-homes-at-end.html (accessed 17. May 2015.)

[13] Cooney, A. and Murphy, K. (2009) 'Ethos of care and environment in long-stay care setting: impacts on residents' lives', in R. Edmondson and H-J. Kondratowitz (eds) *Valuing older people: A humanist approach to ageing,* Bristol: Policy Press.

[14] Victor, C. (2015).

[15] Breeze, E. and Lang, I. (2008) 'Physical functioning in a community context', in J. Banks, E. Breeze, C. Lessof and J. Nazroo (eds) *Living in the 21st century: Older people in England*, London: Institute for Fiscal Studies.

[16] Banks, J., Nazroo, J. and Steptoe, A. (eds) (2012) *The dynamics of ageing: Evidence from the English Longitudinal Study of Ageing 2002–10*, London: Institute for Fiscal Studies.

[17] Larsson, K., Silverstein, M. and Thorslund, M. (2005) 'Delivering care to older people at home', in M. Johnson (ed) *The Cambridge handbook of age and ageing*, Cambridge: Cambridge University Press.

[18] Canadian Health Services Research Foundation (2011) 'Mythbusters', *Eurohealth*, vol 17, no 1, pp 20–21.

[19] Beach, B. and Bamford, S. (2014) *Isolation: the emerging crisis for older men*, London: International Longevity Centre.

[20] Cooney, A. and Murphy, K. (2009).

[21] Independent Commission on Improving Urgent Care for Older People (2016) *Growing old together: Sharing new ways to support older people*, NHS Confederation.

[22] ILC-UK (2016)*Tomorrow's world: The future of ageing in the UK*, www.ilcuk.org.uk/index.php/publications/publication_details/tomorrows_world_the_future_of_ageing_in_the_uk (accessed 14 February 2016.)

Chapter Eleven

[1] ONS (2016) 'At what age is personal well-being the highest?', www.ons.gov.uk (accessed 07 February 2016.)

2   Burkeman, O. (2015) 'Don't fear the reaper', *Guardian*, 29 May.

3   Public Health England (2013) *What we know now, 2013*, London: Public Health England.

4   Public Health England (2013).

5   Winter, D. (2013) 'At the end of the day', Abingdon: The Bible Reading Fellowship.

6   Gawande, A. (2014) *Being mortal*, London: Profile Books, p 154.

7   Phillips, J., Ajrouch, K. and Hillcoat-Nalletamby, S. (2010) *Key concepts in social gerontology*, London: Sage.

8   Age UK (2015a) *Later life in the United Kingdom,* London: Age UK.

9   Alzheimer's Society (2011) 'Dementia people's biggest fear in later life', https://www.alzheimers.org.uk/site/scripts/news_article.php?newsID=907 (accessed 15 February 2016).

10   Alzheimer's Society (2014) *Dementia UK: Update*, https://www.alzheimers.org.uk/site/scripts/download_info.php?fileID=2323 (accessed 15 February 2016).

11   Alzheimer's Society (2014).

12   Devlin, H. (2015) 'Two drugs may halt Alzheimer's, trial suggests', *Guardian*, 1 July.

13   ILC-UK (2016) *Tomorrow's world: The future of ageing in the UK*, www.ilcuk.org.uk/index.php/publications/publication_details/tomorrows_world_the_future_of_ageing_in_the_uk (accessed 14 February 2016.)

14   Murray, K. (2013) 'The communities driving through change for people with dementia', *Guardian,* 11 December.

15   Alzheimer's Society (2013) 'Record numbers of people with dementia in care homes', https://www.alzheimers.org.uk/site/scripts/news_article.php?newsID=1498 (accessed 15 February 2016).

16   Beach, B. and Bamford, S.-M. (2014) *Isolation: The emerging crisis for older men*, London: ILC-UK

17   Beach, B. and Bamford, S.-M. (2014).

18   Bolton, M. (2012) *Loneliness – the state we're in,* Oxfordshire: Age UK, www.campaigntoendloneliness.org/wp-content/uploads/Loneliness-The-State-Were-In.pdf (accessed 19 October 2015.)

19   Seccombe, I. (2016) 'How to work together to beat loneliness', *Guardian,* 4 February.

20   Age UK (2015b) 'Later life in the United Kingdom', www.ageuk.org.uk/Documents/EN-GB/Factsheets/Later_Life_UK_

factsheet.pdf?dtrk=true (accessed 2 November 2015.) [is this the same document as is referenced in note 8?]

[21] Eurostat (nd) *Adequacy and sustainability of pensions*, http://ec.europa.eu/europe2020/pdf/themes/04_pensions.pdf (accessed 11 November 2015.)

[22] Hill, K., Sutton, L. and Hirsch, D. (2011) *Living on a low income in later life*, London: Age UK.

[23] Burkeman (2015).

Chapter Twelve

[1] Roberts, Y. (2012) *One hundred not out: Resilience and active ageing*, London: The Young Foundation.

[2] Rogers, C. (1980) *A way of being*. Boston, MA: Houghton Mifflin Co.

[3] Nathanson. G. (2012) 'Student aged 78 gets an education worth waiting for', *Guardian*, 28 November, guardian.co.uk www.guardian.co.uk/education/mortarboard/2012/nov/28/student-78-gets-an-education-worth-waiting-for (accessed 27 January 2015).

[4] Russell, M. and Simanowitz, V. (2013) 'Retirement or renaissance?', *Therapy Today*, vol 24, no 2, p 16.

[5] Phillips, J. (2010) 'Other lives', *Guardian*, 31 July, p 35.

[6] Thomas, D. (2014) 'Tech industry taps into surge of ageing baby boomers surfing the net', *Guardian*, 27 October, p 23.

[7] Damodaran, L. (2012) *Promoting digital participation*, Loughborough: Loughborough University Press.

[8] Hallam, S., Creech, A., Gaunt, H., Pincas, A., Varvarigou, M. and McQueen, H. (2011) *Music for Life project: The role of participation in community music activities in promoting social engagement and well-being in older people*, London: New Dynamics of Ageing.

[9] Giddens, A. (1991) *Modernity and self-identity*, Cambridge: Polity Press, p 54.

[10] McAdams, D.P. (1993) *The stories we live by: Personal myths and the making of the self*, New York: Morrow.

[11] Athill, D. (2015) *Alive, alive oh!*, London: Granta Books, p 2.

[12] *Independent* (2015) 'Sir Mick Jagger and the great-grandparent club: why more of us will know our children's children's children', 18 August.

[13] Keizer, R. (2011) 'Childlessness and norms of familial responsibility in the Netherlands', *Journal of Comparative Family Studies*, vol 1, no 424, pp 421–38.

[14] Athill, D. (2012) 'I'd much rather have a puppy', *Weekend Guardian*, 17 November, p 62.

[15] Stretch, E. and Cusak, B. (2015) 'World's Oldest Newlyweds', *Mirror*, pp 1 and 9.

[16] Johnson, S. (2015) 'I thought I would never marry again, but I found love at the age of 80', *Guardian*, www.theguardian.com/society/2015/feb/11marry (accessed 25 March 2015).

[17] Harries, E. and de Las Casas, L. (2013) *Who will love me, when I'm 64? The importance of relationships in later life,* London: Relate.

[18] Stephenson Connolly, P. (2010) 'Sex after 50', *Guardian, Life and Style*, www.guardian.co.uk/lifestyle/2010/aug/10/sex-after-50 (accessed 12 September 2015).

[19] ONS (2015) *Families and households*, www.gov.uk/government (accessed 10 July 2015).

[20] Coleman, P.G., Ivani-Chalina, C. and Robinson, M. (1998) 'The story continues: persistence of life themes in old age', *Ageing and Society*, vol 18, no 4, pp 389–419.

[21] Neugarten, B. (1968) 'Adult personality: toward a psychology of the lifecourse', in B. Neugarten (ed) *Middle age and aging*, Chicago: University of Chicago Press, pp 3–37.

[22] Humphrey, A. and Scott, A. (2012) *Older people's use of concessionary bus travel*, NatCen, prepared for Age UK, www.natcen.ac.uk/media/28438/concessionary-bus-travel.pdf (accessed 21 August 2015).

[23] Ruskin, S. (2010) 'The perfect age ... 74?', *Guardian, Life and Style*, www.guardian.co.uk/lifestyle/2010/may/08/happiest (accessed 10 June 2015).

[24] Warren, L. and Clarke, A. (2009) '"Woo-hoo, what a ride!" Older people, life stories and active ageing', in R. Edmondson and H.J. von Kondratowitz (eds) *Valuing older people: A humanist approach to ageing*, Bristol: Policy Press, p 244.

[25] Ruskin, S. (2010).

[26] ONS (2016) *At what age is personal well-being the highest?*, London: Office for National Statistics.

[27] Warren, L. and Clarke, A. (2009), p 244.

Chapter Thirteen

[1] Harter, A.C. (2004) '8', in C. Peterson and M.E.P. Seligman, (eds) *Character, strengths and virtues: A handbook and classification*, Oxford: Oxford University Press, pp 181–96.

[2] Garland, R. (1996) *The Greek way of life*, London: Duckworth.

[3] Payne, T. (2015) *The ancient art of growing old*, London: Vintage, pp 69 and 73.

[4] Sternberg, R. and Grigorenko, E. (2005) 'Intelligence and wisdom', in M.L. Johnson (ed) *The Cambridge handbook of age and ageing*, Cambridge: Cambridge University Press.

[5] Edmondson, R. (2009) 'Wisdom: a humanist approach to valuing older people', in R. Edmondson and H.J. von Kondratowitz (eds) *Valuing older people: A humanist approach to ageing*, Bristol: Policy Press, pp 202–5.

[6] Kenyon, G. (1988) 'Basic assumptions in theories of human aging,' in J. Birren and Y. Bengtson (eds) *Emergent theories of aging*, New York: Springer Publishing Co.

[7] Randall, W. and Kenyon, G. (2000) *Ordinary wisdom: Biographical aging and the journey of life*, Engelska, Greenwood Press.

[8] Edmondson, R. (2009), p 208.

[9] Edmondson, R. (2009), pp 202–5.

[10] Edmondson, R. (2009), p 206.

[11] Harter, A.C. (2004).

[12] Mercer, N. (2000) *Words and minds: How we use language to think together*, London: Routledge.

[13] Jones, I.R., Leontowitsch, M. and Higgs, P. (2010) 'The experience of retirement in second modernity', http://soc.sagepub.com/content/44/1/103 (accessed 23 March 2011).

[14] Eldering Institute (2009–11) 'Wisdom in action – eldering principles', http://ca.eldering.org/eldering/principles (accessed 4 November 2015).

[15] Edmondson, R. (2015) *Ageing, insight and wisdom: Meaning and practice across the lifecourse*, Bristol: Policy Press.

[16] Harter, A.C. (2004).

[17] Diamond, J. (2012) *The world until yesterday: What can we learn from traditional families*, London: Allen Lane, chapter 6, 'The treatment of old people. Cherish, abandon or kill?'

[18] See www.goodworkfoundation.org

[19] See www.the guardian.com/education/2015/aug/02/sugata-mitra-school-in-the-cloud.

[20] Roberts, Y. (2012) *One hundred not out: Resilience and active ageing*, London: The Young Foundation, p 52.

Chapter Fourteen

[1] Benn, T. (2013) *A blaze of autumn sunshine. The last diaries*, London: Hutchinson.

[2] Segal, L. (2013) *Out of time: The pleasures and the perils of ageing*, London: Verso.

[3] Karpf, A. (2014) *How to age. The school of life*, Basingstoke: Pan Macmillan.

[4] hooks, b. (2000) *Feminism is for everybody: Passionate politics*, London: Pluto Press.

[5] Crawshaw, S. and Jackson, J. (2010) *Small acts of resistance: How courage, tenacity, and ingenuity can change the world*, New York and London: Union Square Press.

[6] Andrews, M. (1991) *Lifetimes of commitments*, Cambridge: Cambridge University Press.

[7] Andrews, M. (1991), p 171.

[8] Karpf, A. (2014), p 135.

[9] Karpf, A. (2014), p 133.

[10] Couvee, K. (2015) 'People call you dear and then treat you like an idiot', *Islington Tribune*, 5 June, p 3.

[11] For the full list go to www.bookword.co.uk.

[12] Petty, M. (2015) 'Local heroes', *Saga Magazine*, June, pp 52–9.

[13] For updates, see friendsofblencathra.co.uk.

[14] Karpf, A. (2014), p 136.

Index